Sekai Nzenza-Shand was born in Zimbabwe. She trained as a registered nurse in England before moving to Australia in 1985, where she studied political science and completed a PhD in international relations at the University of Melbourne. Her first novel, *Zimbabwean Woman: My Own Story*, was published in London in 1988, and her fiction has been included in the short stories collections *Daughters of Africa* and *Images of the West*. Sekai currently lives in Zimbabwe.

SONGS TO AN AFRICAN SUNSET

A ZIMBABWEAN STORY

Sekai Nzenza-Shand

LONELY PLANET PUBLICATIONS
Melbourne • Oakland • London • Paris

Songs to an African Sunset: A Zimbabwean Story

Published by Lonely Planet Publications
Head Office: PO Box 617, Hawthorn, Vic 3122, Australia
Branches: 155 Filbert St, Suite 251, Oakland, CA 94607, USA
10 Barley Mow Passage, Chiswick, London W4 4PH, UK
71 bis rue du Cardinal Lemoine, 75005 Paris, France

Published 1997

Printed by SNP Printing Pte Ltd, Singapore

Author photograph by John Gould
Map by Michelle Stamp

This project has been assisted by the Commonwealth
Government through the Australia Council, its arts
funding and advisory body.

National Library of Australia Cataloguing in Publication Data

Nzenza-Shand, Sekai
Songs to an African sunset: a Zimbabwean story.

ISBN 0 86442 472 8.

1. Nzenza-Shand, Sekai – Journeys – Zimbabwe.
2. Zimbabwe – Description and travel.
3. Zimbabwe – Social life and customs.
I. Title. (Series: Journeys (Hawthorn, Vic.).)

919.6891051

In memory of my brother Charles Zororo Nzenza.
He made me come home.

ACKNOWLEDGMENTS

Many people have helped me in different ways during the writing of this narrative. I am deeply grateful to my large extended family in Zimbabwe, Australia and the US for inspiring me with stories of their everyday life experiences. In particular, I would like to thank my children Kudzai and Julian for sharing the struggles and excitement of living between African and Western cultures. I also wish to thank World Vision Australia for offering me the opportunity of visiting and working in remote parts of Zimbabwe. Finally, I want to extend my gratitude to my husband, Adam Shand, and son Jack for accompanying me on the journey back home.

CONTENTS

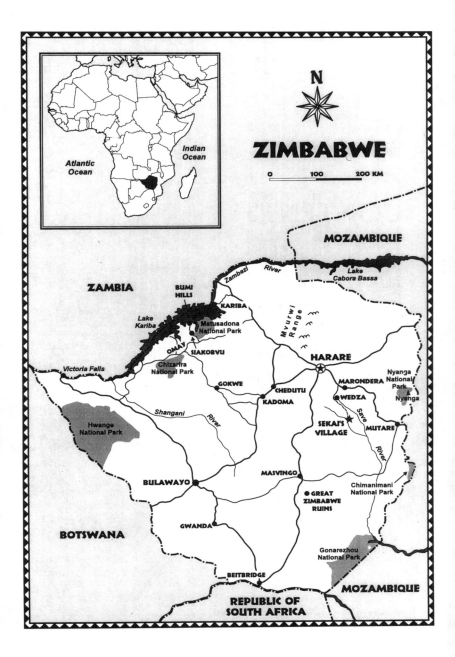

CHAPTER 1

Who Will Bury Us?

IT WAS ONE of those spectacular postcard images: the Zimbabwean sun was slowly turning into a huge red ball on the horizon. Everything around us glowed as we jumped over puddles of water, following the narrow path through tall green grass.

On either side of the path, the fields were full of a promising harvest. After three years of drought, the rains had come as a most valued blessing. No-one would starve this year or be forced to line up for drought relief handouts from benevolent Western governments. It had been a good year.

As she walked, my mother commented cheerfully to my sister and me on the height of her neighbours' maize and sorghum and sunflowers. It was beautiful country. Memories of my childhood flooded my thoughts, just as the sunset bathed the granite boulders on the nearby hillside.

I was born under the ministrations of two village mid-wives in a hut which once stood amongst those rocks. That was long before my parents moved away from the main village and established their own corrugated-iron-roofed house up the hill, away from everyone else. But my mother never stopped going to the main village, whether for a social visit or an important meeting. And we children used to come back from boarding school and go swimming in the river with the village children.

Living in Australia, I had treasured sweet memories of the village and longed to return to it – just to see the old folks again. Now I was going back. The beauty of the place had not changed. But an intense sadness hung above the peaceful valley: we were on our way to my cousin Patrick's funeral.

Suddenly Amai stopped pointing at the green fields. She quickened her pace and started to moan softly. As we approached the main village, she gradually raised her voice, then broke into a loud wailing and ran towards the funeral gathering. "*Tovigwa naniko? Tovigwa naniko?*" she cried. "Who will bury us? Who will bury us?" My aunt, Patrick's mother, came forward to embrace Amai. She had no voice left to mourn her son.

All night I sat with the women around the fire in the big kitchen hut. Every now and again Patrick's mother's husky voice would rise, mourning the death of her son. Someone would start to sing a religious song, and everyone would join in until the hymn became drowned by tears.

Outside, the men sat around a dying fire, weeping silently.

Just before sunrise, my mother told the women that she had to accompany my sister and me to the bus stop. Two days later I was sitting on a Qantas 747 on my way to Australia, but my thoughts were back at the village. I could see all those people I had known since my childhood. They kept echoing my mother's mourning wail: "Who will bury us?" Amai had spoken not just for Patrick's mother or for herself, but for parents the whole world over.

▲▲▲

Patrick was twenty-four years old when he died. Although I had last seen him twelve years before, I had vivid memories of him as a handsome, bright boy. He had grown up to be the pride of his parents, and at twenty-two was a school-teacher with a promising future. The whole family looked to Patrick for financial assistance; on his own salary alone, my uncle could not afford to pay for the education of his eight other children.

When Patrick had come home the previous Christmas, his parents had expected him to return to the small town of Masvingo where he had been teaching for the past two years. But Patrick did not go back after term started. He told his parents that he was sick. He started drinking heavily and smoking village-grown marijuana. His parents could not understand what had befallen their son. Then he started coughing and losing weight, and gradually he refused to be seen by people. My mother had visited him in January and she said he looked like an emaciated old man. She suspected that Patrick had caught the new city disease called *hedzi*.

Everyone was talking about this new killer disease, but not many people in the village knew much about it except that it was transferred sexually by prostitutes and urban men who were isolated from their rural wives. They saw this *hedzi* as a severe kind of gonorrhoea without any known cure. Any illness associated with sex or sexual organs was called *sicky* and was treated by traditional healers without being openly discussed, as it is taboo to talk about sex.

Patrick's parents could not believe that their mission-educated boy could have been sleeping with prostitutes. They felt that if this *hedzi* existed, it should affect other people – surely not their handsome boy. They started to believe that their son had had an evil spell cast on him by someone in the village or someone jealous of his success. For weeks they hid Patrick inside the house, and then one night they took him on a bus to Murambinda, 100 kilometres away, where there was a rural hospital. Two days later the nurses told them that Patrick had advanced AIDS-related tuberculosis and did not have long to live.

My uncle and aunt hired a car and had Patrick dropped off a few kilometres away from the village. At night they wheeled him home down a rocky hill in a wheelbarrow so that no-one they knew would see him in his terminal state. "He's got malaria," they told close relatives.

Patrick knew exactly what was wrong with him. But he could not talk to his parents about it because he felt guilty for having failed them. He called his mother in to him in his final hours and asked for forgiveness. "If only I had a wife and a child to be remembered by," he said to her. Yet to have had a wife and a child in his position would only have meant they were at risk from AIDS.

"How can I die so young?" Patrick asked his mother, then put his head on her lap like a little child, and died. It was early morning and there were just the two of them together. My aunt told my mother that she did not cry. She said that she was angry – angry with the evil forces that could take a young man in his prime.

A few days before Patrick died, the elders of the village went to consult a *n'anga*, a traditional healer with psychic powers, about the cause of the young man's illness. "There is a man in your village who keeps a *chikwambo* that is responsible for Patrick's death," said the *n'anga*. The elders knew that he had to be referring to Uncle Mujubheki; he was the only person in the village who had anything that might be a *chikwambo*, a strange object with magical properties that could cause harm.

My mother told me that the elders called everyone together to hear what the *n'anga* had said. Uncle Mujubheki was then summoned before the people. He was a skinny man of about seventy. He wore ancient overalls with several patches at the knees and a pair of black gumboots. His old clothes were spotless: it was clear that he could not tolerate dirt. He smoked a pipe which he periodically chewed or sucked as he tried to defend himself against the accusation.

"Sirs, in 1945 I left this village for the big city of Salisbury. For a few months I worked as a tea boy for a government department. Then I met Mr Van Riebeck, a Boer from South Africa, who offered me employment as a cook in Johannesburg. I was in Johannesburg for ten years, and then I moved to Cape Town where I worked as a cook for a Mr Jones. I met a Zulu woman and had my three children with her. She met another man and left me to care for the children. I thought I was never going to come back home. But from 1975 to 1979, I had terrible dreams in which my late father appeared and asked me to come home. After consulting a *n'anga* about this dream, I was advised to come back here. But there is a war in Rhodesia, I told the *n'anga*. He said that there were wars everywhere in Africa. So I was not safe in South Africa. 'If you should die, go and die among your people,' the *n'anga* said.

"I loved Cape Town but the dreams of my father could not let me rest. I made all the necessary arrangements and gave notice to my employer. The night before I left Cape Town I went for a walk on the beach. I felt very lonely and isolated because I knew that I was unlikely to return. So I got a bottle and filled it with sea water, and then I pulled up some seaweed and put it in the bottle. I comforted myself with the belief that the smell of the sea and the seaweed would remind me of Cape Town. Thirty years in South Africa is a long time. I have been here for fifteen years but I still dream of the beautiful Zulu women, the gumboot dances, the bare mountains and the mist covering them – and, of course, of the sea."

Uncle Mujubheki's face looked full of sorrow. Everyone was watching him but no-one spoke until one of the elders asked him to tell the people about his *chikwambo*.

"I was about to get to that," said Uncle Mujubheki. "Back home, I found it terribly hard to settle into these village routines. Whenever I thought of Cape Town, I would go into the granary where I keep my suitcase, take out my bottle of sea water and smell the seaweed. Over the years, I have started to believe that the smell of the sea is very healthy to one's body. Since I returned from South Africa, I have not spent one day in bed because of ill health. Some people here may remember my narrow escape from being killed by the white soldiers during the war. Let me tell you that I escaped because that very morning when a bullet went over my head, I had drunk a mouthful of sea water.

"But of course, some people are jealous and suspicious of me, and they have created a story saying that my bottle is an evil *chikwambo* so that it will be destroyed. But my sea water is not a symbol of witchcraft. It is not a *chikwambo*. How can people want to rob me of something so innocent and so simple?"

The elders asked Uncle Mujubheki to fetch the bottle, which he did. He held it up and showed it to the people. By that time the *n'anga* had arrived; he ordered the crowd to move away so he could destroy the bottle himself. Everyone watched as the bottle was smashed against a stone and brown sea water soaked into the red earth.

Although Uncle Mujubheki knew that Patrick had AIDS, he did not say so to the elders. How could he, when he was hiding his own son Stephen's illness?

Stephen did not attend Patrick's funeral because he was suffering from severe chest pains and mouth ulcers and was too sick to travel to the village from Harare. He was being treated at a clinic in the city where no-one knew him. I visited him the day before I flew back to Australia.

He laughed sadly when I told him about the bottle of sea water. "It's only a bottle of water, and they all know it." But the problem, he went on to say, was that his father himself had begun to believe that the bottle had extraordinary powers. So with Patrick's untimely death, it had been easy for other people in the village to believe that the innocent bottle of sea water was a magical fetish.

Stephen had very little education, but he was street-wise and he knew that Patrick had died of AIDS. He had been very close to his cousin, and Patrick and he had often spent time together in the city as well as in the village. They had had girlfriends they had grown up with in the country and others they had met in the city; Stephen knew that their chances of contracting *sicky* were quite high. He also knew that some of his other friends, former freedom fighters, had already died from or were showing signs of AIDS. The nurses at the Harare clinic had told him that sexually transmitted diseases increased vulnerability to the virus. He had also been told that in the West the disease mainly affected homosexuals and drug addicts. However, like most people in the village, Stephen knew almost nothing about either of these; homosexuality was common in prison but not among village boys.

Despite everything he knew about AIDS, Stephen told me that when he got better and returned to the village, he was not going to talk about the disease; to do so would bring more shame to his father. And so the conspiracy of silence about AIDS continued.

◢▲◣

The nearest health centre to our village was ten kilometres away and it was staffed by only one state-enrolled nurse and an assistant. Even if condoms were available at the centre, village women with husbands in the city would not like to be seen buying them in case they were accused of adultery.

Those who needed condoms most were the sexually active men like Patrick and Stephen. Unfortunately, most of them were unemployed and could not afford contraceptives. These young men, and also women, would spend short periods looking for work in the city, then come back to the village with a few dollars in their pocket and the HIV virus.

Constance, one of my older sisters, was a trained nurse and an AIDS counsellor. She tried to tell Patrick's parents that AIDS was a very serious and dangerous disease and that there was no need to blame anyone for it, least of all a bottle of sea water; all that was needed to do after Patrick's death was to be sympathetic and supportive towards each other. But she was trying to counsel people who were not ready for counselling. The denial process was not over and Patrick's parents, like the other people in the village, were still a long way away from understanding the disease.

There is a strong belief among the Shona people that an illness or death does not occur without reason: misfortunes are caused by evil from within or from outside. For instance, a past misadventure by an ancestor could bring ill-fortune to the present generation if those old sins have not been atoned for. According to this traditional philosophy, the spirit of someone who might have been murdered or simply ill-treated by someone from Patrick's family could have been behind his death, even if the immediate cause of his death had been acknowledged to be a disease. In other words, a child might suffer as a result of the sins committed by his parents or even their parents before them – a belief that reinforces family and social ties.

There are other reasons too why people look beyond the rational to explain *hedzi*. In times of social change, people become insecure and anxious; to find an explanation for extraordinary events they search for scapegoats such as Uncle Mujubheki's bottle of sea water. History tells us that witch-hunting is a phenomenon of severe crises in society, and traditional values are undergoing rapid change in Zimbabwe. The extended family is fragmenting as young people search for individual identity in the cities, away from their villages.

Even at national level, the present is seen as chaotic and the past as orderly and romantic. The vice-president of the country, Dr Joshua Nkomo, once ordered the banning of a television advertisement encouraging the use of condoms and said that the ad was a national disgrace. He saw this method of sex education designed to prevent the spread of AIDS as immoral and argued that it only encouraged young people to have pre-marital sex.

One of Dr Nkomo's sons died of the disease in 1996. At least Dr Nkomo had the courage to announce in the press that it was AIDS that took his son, rather than the mysterious 'long illness' that seems to be sweeping the higher echelons of the country. But he described AIDS as a Western invention sent to keep Africans down. So much for rational debate about the disease in Zimbabwe.

Two years after Patrick died, my brother Charles fell victim to AIDS. After five years spent working in West Germany, Charles had returned to Zimbabwe with his family, ready to take advantage of his training and experience with Air Zimbabwe. By the time he was forty he was already a successful man, with several BMWs and Mercedes Benz, his own printing business and acres of land.

However, it turned out there was little to celebrate on his return, when the symptoms of the disease began to manifest themselves. The slide that every HIV sufferer must dread had begun. Charles's physical strength began to ebb, as if his body had decided to accommodate the virus. He gradually lost weight and went through two hospitalisations, without fuss or self-pity. One day, stretched out in the back of his black Mercedes, Charles was driven by Rudo, his wife, to see a *n'anga*; the traditional healer prescribed elixirs which proved as useless as they were expensive.

From a little flower shop in Melbourne, my sisters and I sent Charles huge bouquets wishing him better health. For the four years of his illness he had never discussed his condition with the family, and so we continued the fiction that he would recover. Already, one of Charles's girlfriends had died; another would later fall ill.

My three sisters who lived in Harare, my mother, Rudo and Rudo's grandmother nursed Charles and comforted him. When tuberculosis and pneumonia took over, we knew that our brother had lost the battle. Night after night we waited for the phone call from Harare that would tell us the inevitable.

When his doctor said there was nothing further medical aid could do, Charles said he preferred to die at home. He died in the early hours of the morning in his own bed, next to his wife, with Amai sleeping on the floor nearby. In the cool suburban dawn, my mother walked around Charles's garden; her voice could be heard calling upon the ancestral spirits to come down and give her the strength to mourn her son. Then she called the names of all her children to tell them that the water had been spilt. No-one could comfort her at that moment. For several hours, they left her alone until her voice and energy were exhausted.

Two days later, my sisters and I boarded the plane that would take us from Melbourne to Harare. When we arrived at Charles's house he was lying peacefully in his front room surrounded by hundreds of mourners. Amai sat by and looked on without emotion – she could no longer cry. The pain of losing her forty-year-old son was too much to bear. The despair on my mother's face is something I shall never forget.

As is the custom, my brother was to be buried in the village and not in a public urban cemetery; he was to stay close to his ancestors as he had requested in his will. We travelled home to the village in convoy that night. Everyone I had known from the days of my childhood was there.

While most people mourned and grieved with us, a group of thirty women from my mother's village laughed, mocked us and danced. These women were called *varoora*, which means daughters-in-law. They had no blood relationship to Charles, but they had married my mother's brothers, nephews and cousins and had become part of the maternal extended family. In her maiden village, my mother was looked on as the great aunt, or an honorary man; the *varoora* gave her the respect due to a father and my mother could command them as she wished. They therefore came to their 'husband's' village to support her in her bereavement. Their role was not only to sing and dance, but also to cook meals and feed all the mourners. Because they were not known in my mother's village, they could tease anyone and take the role of clowns in order to lighten the spirits of the people, mocking the seriousness of death.

Among the *varoora* were Catholics, Anglicans, Methodists and followers of other faiths as well. Yet they all sang the same traditional songs in one voice as if they had been trained to do so. These songs had never been written down but the women could easily switch from one song to the next.

The night before my brother was to be buried, I sat near the coffin. There were no men in this hut. I sat with my mother, my sisters, Rudo and Charles's four girlfriends. It was a known fact that Charles loved women and that he had ten children by three women. The *varoora* sang about his womanising with great mirth. Role-plays about Charles and his girlfriends were acted out right in front of the coffin. I remember a sketch in which one woman dressed up in Charles's clothes while another *varoora* pretended to be his city sweetheart.

"Where do you fancy going, darling?" asked the woman who was Charles.

"The executive suite at the Sheraton," replied the other.

"No problem, my love. But would you rather go for a drive to the lake?"

"Whatever you wish, as long as your wife does not know about this. Otherwise, she will kill herself from jealousy."

"No she won't. She is used to it. She knows I am an African man and a man like me with lots of money should have several wives. That is my right," said the woman playing Charles, puffing out her chest.

Then the *varoora* hugged and pretended to get into an expensive car. My mother laughed, as did Charles's wife and the two of his girlfriends who were also mothers of his children. There was no jealousy or ill-feeling between my sister-in-law and these women.

Throughout the night we sang, we cried and we danced. At dawn my mother walked around her front yard, calling Charles's name across the small homestead where he grew up. All the women joined in her mourning song: "*Kwayedza Charles. Kwayedza chimuka.*" "It is dawn, Charles. It is dawn. Wake up." It was as if Charles would suddenly bound out of the old house, ready to walk to school or go off to herd the cattle. The *varoora* were allowing my mother to 'wake up' her son for the last time. When her mourning song had dissolved into a hoarse wail, they led her back into the hut. Then they offered her warm water to bathe herself and set about making tea. After feeding her and making sure that she was calm, they began to prepare tea for all the mourners and all the men camped outside.

Four days after his death, Charles was laid beside his father on a rocky slope by the track to the homestead, protected by a pair of thorn trees. His grave looked out over high craggy plains to the horizon. As we walked away from the grave, rain began to fall, despite the fact that Zimbabwe was then in the grip of its worst drought in years. The old people said that the gentle shower had been sent by the ancestral spirits to wash Charles's footprints from this earth, in preparation for his journey into the next.

After the funeral, most of our relatives returned to their villages. Rudo, my sisters and I stayed with Amai for a few more days. Then we all left and I went back to Melbourne. But in my mind I could see the faces of the *varoora* singing and dancing, accompanying my brother with their songs to the land of the unknown.

Who knew who would be next? With Charles gone, who

would be able to bring sugar, bread and vegetables to my mother? Was this the end of the homestead, with just my sad mother and my older brother Sydney living on there amongst the barren remains of our childhood? These questions continuously repeated themselves in my mind. Moving along the aisles in Safeway or browsing in bookshops around Melbourne, I would suddenly feel the need to go back to the village. I knew that I had to make a decision about where I was going to live.

For nearly fourteen years I had lived outside Zimbabwe, first in England and later in Australia. Although I had gone home on holiday at least every two years, I was beginning to see myself as an outsider – someone who did not belong there any more. Yet I did not feel I belonged in multicultural Australia either.

In Melbourne, I had once joined a women's co-operative where I was identified as an NESB, which stood for Non-English Speaking Background. But I did not want labels. What my Australian women friends did not know was that I started learning to speak English on my father's lap, long before teachers at the mission school taught me how to behave like a 'civilised' English person. I did not view myself as an NESB and I really did not like being called ethnic, black or disadvantaged; I was just myself, wanting desperately to be an Australian.

At Melbourne University, where I was studying for a doctorate in international relations, my supervisor and I got on extremely well. We shared and discussed the politics of race, sex and representation. For a couple of years, I even thought I was an intellectual, talking about deconstructionist theory and post-colonialism with academic friends over bottles of good wine.

But I also worried that somehow these people felt privileged to have me around because, in their eyes, I was different and exotic.

I had married an Australian. Sometimes I could ignore all the doubts, and simply be invigorated by the fact that I had penetrated Western society and was able to socialise with our rich yuppie friends. But questions about my background always came up, especially at moments when I felt that I was just another Australian. *What is Africa like? Do you go back to your village? How many people live in the village? What is African food like? Do they believe in God over there? Is there much to eat? Have you got many brothers and sisters? How long since you last went there? How far is Zimbabwe from Rwanda?*

When I announced that I was returning to Zimbabwe to live, the general assumption was that I had decided to go back to my country and was dragging poor Adam with me. Wherever we went, there were more and more questions. I answered them as patiently as I could, and listened to the responses. *Wow, it's great that you're going back to your country. Oh, I wish I could come with you to see the lions and the elephants. I have always loved Africa. May I come and stay with you if I ever decide not to go to Bali? Your mother will be really pleased to have you back.*

In Sydney, we had drinks with my in-laws and their wealthy Rose Bay and Double Bay friends. The smartly dressed couples congratulated Adam for being adventurous and different. "Not many young men from your kind of background would do that, you know," they said. Adam's parents were clearly proud of him but his brother and sisters were ambivalent about his decision. As I made polite conversation, I could hear Adam's voice: "Zimbabwe is a beautiful country and quite safe. No, there are no warring tribesmen. The Shona and the Ndebele have signed a peace accord and everything is peaceful now. The white people who stayed after independence are really doing very well economically. In fact, they're controlling the mining, farming and industrial sectors of the economy." Those guests who had been to Zimbabwe believed him, but those who had only seen TV images of Africa laughed gently and walked away.

They were nice and kind to me, but these rich people from Sydney's eastern suburbs did not know my world. As a good daughter-in-law, I spoke politely to them and answered questions covering the whole African continent. *No, I did not speak Zulu. Yes, I learnt to speak English when I was quite young. Yes, Shona and Zulu were related but Shona did not have the click sound. Yes, AIDS was a serious problem in Africa and no, Nigeria was really quite far from Zimbabwe.*

In Zimbabwe no-one would ask me questions about my hair, my food, my dress, where I was from and when I would be going back. At times in Australia I felt I was in a museum where people could gaze at me and ask questions. Being black, African and a woman was enough for people to feel that they could ask about my personal life in public. Going back to Zimbabwe meant that I would be anonymous.

And I would no longer be subjected to questions about Ethiopian famine, Nigerian dictatorship, South African post-apartheid unrest and Rwandan tribal violence. To some Australians, Africa was one big country and they assumed that all Africans living in Australia knew each other. I remember attending a party in Balmain once, where a middle-aged lady asked me if I knew Ike from Nigeria. If I did not know Ike, then surely I must know Kwaku from Ghana? She was rather disappointed when I said I had never met either of these people. Then she asked me if I would invite her to an African party so that she could meet some interesting black guys and dance to wild, sexual music. Being an ambassador for the whole African continent was a difficult task.

After several farewell dinners with our friends and relatives in Melbourne and Sydney, Adam and I were ready to go to Zimbabwe with our son Jack. My two school-age children, Kudzai and Julian, would be staying in Melbourne. In the spirit of the extended-family tradition, my sisters were happy to look after them, and they would come to Zimbabwe during school holidays. I had a part-time job working for an Australian aid organisation in Harare, so if Adam's plans for freelance journalism did not succeed, we had something to fall back on.

Deep down, I knew it was mainly my brother Charles's death that made me decide to return to the village. I wanted to comfort my mother as well as return to the tracks I had walked with Charles. Going back to the village was a journey to reclaim something of myself that I had lost during years of living in the West.

CHAPTER 2

Following the Tracks Back

THE ROAD HOME was as difficult as I remembered it, a rough three-hour drive over the corrugations, not helped by the fact that we were travelling in one of Charles's huge old BMWs which could not have been less well adapted to this journey.

Adam was used to driving on rough roads back home in Australia, but I could tell from his expression that he had never seen anything like this before. The road was really only intended for the village buses that plied this route twice a day. It began as a neat, two-lane strip of tar, but that was short-lived; a single-lane tarred stretch continued uncertainly for a while, until abruptly the dusty road took over. You could always tell when you had left the commercial farms owned by the whites because the tarred road and electricity poles would end. After that, you were in the Tribal Trust Lands, now known by the more politically correct title of Communal Lands. The change of name had meant little to the people: it had really just been a case of changing masters.

The BMW did not like the dirt road and nor did my husband. He did not see the magnificent blue of the Wedza mountains, the picture-postcard villages, and the little children running out to greet the car. He only saw the potholes, the jagged rocks and the deep culverts where the rains had turned road into river bed. This was not the honeymoon drive he had in mind. Travelling at thirty kilometres an hour produced vibrations that drowned out the stereo and when, after half an hour, the dashboard fell away in our laps, we had to forget about music altogether. We stopped frequently to clear away rocks or to survey the road ahead, which at every turn potentially concealed axle-snapping obstacles.

Still, we were getting closer to home all the time. Soon we were in sight of the mountain, Dengedza, that overlooked my village; familiar faces appeared on the roadside. The road had become smooth and my husband was clearly enjoying himself now – he was even smiling and commenting on the scenery. I didn't have the heart to tell him about our driveway.

On reflection, it was less a driveway than the result of a rockslide. Not that we stopped to reflect too much when the rock struck the bottom of the car: a big rock all right, but hardly big enough to stand out against the hundreds of others that were scattered across the final 200-metre stretch to the homestead.

Our homecoming was rapturous. I hadn't been back for a while, and my mother ran out from the kitchen to greet us, ululating and dancing, raising dust as she came. My brother Sydney, his wife, Mai Shuvai, and their children heard the commotion and came running up from their huts to see what it was all about. Bathed in the purple light of late afternoon, it was a perfect scene and I felt a peace and happiness that only being home can bring.

Then somebody saw the oil pouring into the red dust underneath our car.

"*Maiweeeeee!*" (My mother!) screeched Mai Shuvai irrelevantly as she tried to stem the flow of hot oil from the sump with cotton wool. The cotton wool was replaced by a tin mug, which quickly overflowed and was replaced with a pot, and then a still bigger one. Soon just about every kitchen utensil was filled with the steaming oil.

To me, this scene had a familiarity about it that if anything made me feel more at home. Life in the village was an ongoing cycle of crisis and resolution. Nothing, except sickness and death, could disturb the overall pattern. As time was rarely an issue, wasting it meant virtually nothing at all; therefore, there was no urgency to find a solution to our problem. This was the art of life in the village.

But for my husband, being 150 kilometres from civilisation with a broken car, no tools and no hope of a passing BMW mechanic was nothing short of a major crisis, an absolute show-stopper. After he finished yelling and kicking the dust, he just sat down and stared into the distance, trying to resign himself to the prospect of an indefinite stay in the village. Here was a person who had never experienced the feeling of being abandoned by twentieth-century technology.

The people in the village did not understand what all the fuss was about. Tomorrow at four in the morning, the bus back to Harare would come by the village, waking everybody with its three-note horn blaring out 'Strangers in the Night'. If the car could not be fixed, the white man could simply get on the bus for the six-hour journey back to town.

Uncle Chakwanda, who had arrived from the main village, appointed himself mechanic to our stricken automobile. He had never fixed anything more complex than a windlass or a paraffin lamp but he led Adam away in search of 'parts' to fix the oil sump. Adam followed him, his shoulders drooping, all his power as a civilised Westerner visibly ebbing away. An hour later the two of them returned with a half-tube of two-part epoxy cement, with which Uncle Chakwanda intended to restore the damage to the pride of German engineering the following morning.

"It will never work. This old man must be bloody crazy," said Adam, laughing without an ounce of mirth. "Has anybody else got a car around here? Maybe there's a farmhouse somewhere that has a phone."

Everybody laughed at the sight of the white man covered in oil and dust, looking wildly around for some sign of hope – an electric light in the distance, an aeroplane flying overhead, some ingenious technology to help him out of his predicament.

▰▰▰

Two or three beers and a bath in the warm water from the borehole lifted Adam's spirits enormously. He and I sat with our backs against the whitewashed wall of my mother's house, watching a huge white moon rise behind the hill, casting long, flat shadows on our little homestead.

Years before, we young girls longed for these full moon nights, when we would meet in the forest, down in the valley far from the kitchen fires, to dance and talk of romance and the future. There were leopards in the forest back then, hidden amongst huge dark trees which stretched out to the horizon. It was wartime and sometimes we would hear the guerillas passing quietly in the scrub, heading into the village to get food, supplies and perhaps the warmth of the older women. We would hold our breath until they passed and then our songs and laughter would slowly start up again, lilting through the trees back to the huts. In that half-light, the faces of my friends had been innocent of the hardships that were to come: teenage motherhood, the decades of drought, long years of war and a revolution which meant very little to rural people.

It would seem that I was among the last children to share the secrets of the forest, the last generation to hope for better things. The forest was virtually gone now. Even the big trees that did remain seemed somehow smaller, twisted and gnarled, their limbs distorted by the yearly harvest of firewood. Where there was once forest there was now just naked earth, cut with erosion gullies which increased with each rainy season. The songs of the village girls had been replaced by the mournful chanting of the white-clad followers of the Apostolic Faith. Times were hard and many people were seeking consolation in this Old Testament-based religion. Perhaps they were looking for the spirits that had disappeared with the forest.

That night, we were to attend an all-night ceremony honouring the spirit of a long-dead ancestor. The *bira* was to be held in the main village, a line of huts towards the river. Walking there with Adam and Sydney, I noticed that the drought winds had seared the chalky soil and that there were no crops in the fields, as there should have been at this time.

As we drew near we could hear the sound of drums and voices coming from the kitchen hut, naturally amplified by the mud bricks and thatch. Groups of men sat outside by fires, drinking *doro*, village beer, a sweet and heady seven-day brew. The drinking of beer has always been a part of Shona life, creating a fellowship between people that cannot be erased by the hardships of life in the village.

People were coming in from all parts for the ceremony, as *biras* were the central social activity in the village – apart from funerals, which seemed to dominate the calendar these days.

Faces of half-forgotten relatives, classmates, neighbours,

domestic workers, teachers came out of the darkness to meet me. Greeting upon greeting was exchanged for more than ten minutes as we moved towards the kitchen hut, where a ragged choir of over thirty married women were singing up a storm by candlelight, in celebration of the ancestor's *mudzimu* or spirit. Three male drummers were pounding out solemn rhythms which from time to time would spontaneously spill into an upbeat tune led by one of the stronger singers.

The air in the small hut was heavy and sensuous – a pervasive smell of body odour and wood smoke enveloped me. Herd boys and schoolgirls drifted past the open door, sneaking looks at the singers. Every so often noted village dancers, both male and female, would bound into the centre of the hut to perform; the rest of us watched them, laughing and singing. Two short planks were passed from hand to hand as clap sticks, to fill out the band.

The villagers were slowly getting used to the fact that Adam was not in fact an albino, as an elderly man had speculated upon our arrival, but my husband from Australia, the one whom my brother Sydney had been bragging about at previous beer sessions. I could imagine Sydney, the village geography teacher with his dirty suit and tie askew, regaling his fellow drinkers with stories about the time he went to Australia to attend our wedding. "We had prawns for supper and ice-cold Australian beer all night. And I danced with white ladies in a very civilised atmosphere!"

Even before his brief Australian trip, Sydney's book-learnt knowledge of the world was unrivalled in the area. Now with his tales of visits to race meetings and red-light sex shops where white women paraded topless in front of him, he was an absolute legend. And besides all that, Sydney had seen the sea, something that virtually none of these men would ever do.

From the darkness came a new group of visitors, walking

purposefully towards the kitchen. The fire-sitters filed in behind these newcomers and I noticed that there was one person at the centre of this procession whom everybody was looking at. The figure was obviously a man but he was dressed in an ill-fitting woman's white gown, like the church ladies used to wear in a bygone era, and his head was covered by a bonnet tied down tight at the sides. He clutched a hatchet which he was waving vigorously, gesturing to his relatives to prepare the way for his return to the family. The appearance of the 'ancestor' on the dance floor visibly affected many of those present, even though the spectre was probably their cousin or uncle. Adam was astonished by the dressed-up man and keen to return to safety, away from the hatchet being waved around.

In Shona culture, someone will dress in the style of a dead person and imitate the mannerisms of this ancestor while dancing, in a ritual that is calculated to awaken the spirit of the dead person in his fellow celebrants. The ceremonies usually last all through the night and are a key element in maintaining village harmony, good seasons and fertility.

The belief in ancestral spirits is woven into village law. Families can demand compensation for wrongs committed long ago to an ancestor by another family; the descendants of people who failed to stop someone being killed in their village are considered guilty of a crime against the ancestors; and a man who insults his mother will face continual bad luck, even after her death, until he puts things right. You ignore the ancestral spirits here at your peril, whatever the white missionary might tell you on Sundays about worshipping idols. People who observe the customs find that the ancestors look after them, as many freedom fighters reported during the war for independence.

The *bira* continues the long dialogue with the ancestors which stretches up to the Great Spirit. The Great Spirit is Mwari, the supreme deity in traditional Shona belief. It is not possible to talk directly to him; people have to ask the ancestors to mediate on their behalf. If Mwari is unhappy about someone's conduct, they ask his forgiveness by paying libations to the ancestral spirits. It is for this reason that Christian missionaries had so much success in Zimbabwe: their sales pitch included unmediated dialogue with God – no more middlemen to go through. Many people found this direct dialling highly appealing.

The beer was still flowing when we began our walk back to the homestead. Sydney was reluctant to leave while the pot was being passed around, but he came with us all the same. As we crossed the fields, he recited a list of developments at his school that Adam and I were to organise by the time of our next visit.

The sky was full of stars, more than my husband had ever seen in the city. "There's a satellite," he said, with great satisfaction.

▲▲▲

My family's village is not really deserving of the name. It is made up of my mother's homestead and my brother Sydney's house, which is down the hill. Sydney stayed in the village so he could teach at the local school, where his wife also teaches. They have six children, three girls at boarding school and three boys still in primary school.

The homestead buildings consist of my mother's grass-thatched hut, and a six-room, corrugated-iron-roofed house; I remember assisting in moulding bricks for this house when I was ten. Then there is the granary and a shelter for our borehole.

Traditionally, our house should have been one of a long line of grass-thatched huts facing a line of sleeping houses. But after my father returned to his village from his teacher training, he and my mother regarded themselves as more civilised than everyone in the main village near the river. So in 1965 they moved up the hill to build a modern house, away from my grandfather and his many wives. For years, this house was the model home in the area, remarked upon for miles because we slept on beds and used pit latrines, which were unknown in most villages at the time.

As children we were required to grow at least one tree each. We grew mangoes, oranges, guavas and lemons. When the trees were in season, Amai had to bury some of the fruit because it all ripened at the same time and could not be preserved.

It was a pleasant, happy home. We mixed with the local kids only at primary school, or when we were herding cattle in the valley or swimming in the river; basically, we kept to ourselves a lot. Our library, housed in my parent's bedroom, was made up of books given to my father by the missionaries. We grew up on authors like Rider Haggard, Enid Blyton, Daniel Defoe, Jules Verne, Rudyard Kipling . . . Our early education about the world came from books like *King Solomon's Mines*, *The Jungle Book*, *The Thirty-Nine Steps*, *Around the World in Eighty Days* and *The Swiss Family Robinson*. As we grew older, we moved on to American pulp fiction such as James Hadley Chase. Mills and Boon romances were a speciality because we could compete with each other on the number of days it took to finish reading 120 pages. In high school we discovered D.H. Lawrence, Charles Dickens and Thomas Hardy. I recall a dog-eared copy of *Lady Chatterley's Lover* being concealed in the granary, as my sisters and I worked our way through its forbidden pages. At night we held quizzes on the classics while sitting around a paraffin lamp near the fire.

As the years went by, one by one we children left the village and pursued careers. But my father died and my mother stayed on, continuing the same duties she had performed for years. Her life appeared to be static. Yet every one of her children who had dreamed of a life beyond the village had had their chance; the achievements of my parents seemed quite remarkable in that respect.

At dawn, I could hear my mother busy in the yard, gathering firewood and water so that the household might have a cup of tea and a plate of porridge before everyone began their chores. I could also hear her domestic helper sweeping the compound free of dust.

Adam and I rose quickly to enjoy the sunrise bursting over the hills across the river, framing the last big *msasa* tree that remained. I couldn't recall the village ever looking so beautiful, despite the ravages of drought and deforestation. Perhaps as a child I had taken it all for granted. I silently thanked my father for firing us children with the ambition to see the world, because to return to the village after a long absence was a chance to see my childhood again.

Uncle Chakwanda arrived after breakfast with his half-tube of epoxy cement and my husband suddenly remembered the mess we were in regarding the car. For the next hour, Uncle Chakwanda daubed the gaping hole in the sump with the cement while Adam looked on, shaking his head. My uncle good-naturedly ignored his comments: "Thanks, but you really are wasting your time, you know." "You have to have an aluminium arc welder to fix something like that on a BMW and all you've got is a tube of goo and a bit of spit." "You've got to be joking. We're never going to get home like this."

While this was going on, I was sitting on a goatskin mat helping my mother and two of the village women to shell groundnuts. I had known these women for a long time; they had not changed much, except that they seemed to be poorer. When they saw me, they only asked my mother which of the girls I was. "The one delivered by Mai Hilda and Mai Keti." The women nodded; they remembered the day I was born. I had an identity in the village – I could not pretend to be anyone else among these people.

In Zimbabwe, people generally speak Shona or Ndebele and, in the case of urban people, fluent English. My mother and her friends were talking in Shona, which was spoken by everyone in the village.

"She was an easy delivery," said Amai.

"Which year was that?"

"The year her grandfather took a fifth wife."

"The epileptic girl from across the Save River?"

"Yes, she bore him five children and then left him for one of the church elders."

"He was too old to perform."

"True, but he never gave up. He married his eighth wife six months before he died."

"What happened to the eighth wife?"

"She came here and asked me if she could be inherited by my husband as his second wife," my mother replied.

"Yes, I remember that," said one of the women. "You told her that your husband was going to marry a second wife. A year later, you brought your niece to be your husband's new wife."

"That's right."

Adam came in to announce that, much to his amazement, the BMW had been fixed. Uncle Chakwanda had produced a battered old tin of motor oil, syphoned from the grinding mill, which was apparently still the only other piece of machinery in the area. Nobody would have their maize ground today, but at least we would get home.

It was a question of faith, living in the village, having a patient attitude and believing that things would work out in the end.

When we picked up our bags to leave, we noticed that a chicken had laid an egg on our pillow. Amai and her friends began to ululate: the egg was a sign that meant Sekai was pregnant. A few weeks later, the doctor confirmed that I was indeed expecting a baby. The chickens are never wrong.

CHAPTER 3

Learning to be Civilised

I AM BACK at Kwenda Methodist Mission after twenty years. My father first attended this school in 1946. Soon after his teacher training here, the Methodist missionaries sent him back to his village with a mission: he was to establish the first school in the area, which he called Mufudzi Wakanaka School – Good Shepherd School. I was born when Baba was still a teacher and a loyal companion to the English missionaries.

But by the early '60s, my father had succumbed to what the missionaries darkly called primitive desires: he became a polygamist. The Reverend Palmer spoke to him earnestly about morality and the oppression of women in polygamous situations. What he did not know was that my father's decision to take a second wife was sanctioned by my mother. Up to this day Amai will maintain that she chose a second wife for my father because he was desperate to prove his manly status and nothing was going to stop him from taking more wives. So my mother went back to her maiden village and brought home her sixteen-year-old niece to be her husband's second wife.

The white missionaries were appalled at my father's conduct. After all the years spent educating him about the value of civilisation and good behaviour, my father had let the mission down. If it was just the question of taking a second wife, they might have forgiven him or pretended not to know. But my father had gone as far as drinking European beer and spirits like vodka and whisky, even though in Rhodesia at the time it was illegal for Africans to drink commercially produced alcohol. And when the Reverend Palmer arrived at the school one Sunday afternoon expecting to find my father preaching to the flock, he was enraged to discover all the village people at a traditional ceremony paying libations to ancestral spirits. To the missionaries' way of thinking, Africans who drank alcohol and worshipped ancestral spirits were primitive and abominable. Polygamy was merely the last straw, proof positive that they had failed to civilise my father.

Baba was summoned to the headmaster's office, where a letter for his dismissal was quickly written out by the Reverend Palmer and presented to him. 'Despite your knowledge of the Lord Jesus and the redemption message, you have chosen to continue worshipping idols and to mislead the natives. You have therefore been found unsuitable to remain as Headmaster of Mufudzi Wakanaka School. Your dismissal takes effect from now.' The Reverend Palmer gave my father two pounds and told him to go home and entertain his two wives.

But his dismissal from teaching did not deter Baba from worshipping ancestral spirits, nor did he divorce his second wife. When we were growing up, he would tell us that if we wanted to be educated and get jobs, we had to obey the white man. In order to be successful in life, Baba would remind us, we should worship the white man's Jesus as well as ancestors and either way we would still get to God. But it was crucial that as we grew up, we should never let the white man know that we worshipped the ancestors.

We all believed in Baba's teaching and we desperately wanted to go to boarding school and learn to speak English as he did. At the age of twelve, Charles, my older sisters and I were sent to the Methodist boarding school at Kwenda Mission. The Reverend Palmer was no longer there. He had gone back to England, leaving the running of the mission to the Mellors, the McClures and Miss Hutchinson. After a year in boarding school I grew to like Miss Hutchinson very much. She epitomised everything I wanted to be: she was intelligent, seemingly wealthy, well fed and a car owner. Her house smelt the way I imagined civilisation to be – fresh and pure, scrubbed clean with wax and detergent.

I did not want to go back to ancestral worship, and the smell of cow dung and poverty in the village. I wrote a letter to Amai telling her about Miss Hutchinson and how much I adored her religion, which I had by then fully embraced. I also told my mother that Baba had been wrong to worship ancestral spirits.

I became Miss Hutchinson's favourite pupil. During my second year in boarding school I confessed that my father was a polygamist, as a result of which we were all very poor. Miss Hutchinson felt sorry for me and the following term she told me that a Methodist Women's Group in Sheffield had offered to pay for my secondary education. I was beginning to enjoy the benefits of being a good Christian, just as my father had done years before.

Miss Hutchinson often looked at me and said, "You are the reason for my coming to Africa." She said that she loved my big white eyes and my clean set of teeth. One day she took a photo of me and said that it would forever remind her that her years of toil in darkest Africa were worthwhile. It was one step towards the kingdom of God, she said. While she talked about the kingdom of God, I was more interested in getting to know about her world.

Miss Hutchinson had lost her fiancé during the Second World War. Then the Lord called her to Africa where she had ended up at Kwenda Mission, teaching agricultural science and maths. Up the hill, a few metres from our dormitory, was her house. She had three bedrooms all to herself and Kim, her faithful black dog.

Between the house and the dormitory were Miss Hutchinson's rabbits. Once a month she paid me and my girlfriend a dollar fifty for killing and skinning a rabbit for her. Killing a rabbit was easy – we would hold its hind legs down with our feet, and then I would hold its front legs and shoulders while my friend cut its throat. Miss Hutchinson watched us from her front doorstep. Soon after we had skinned the rabbit, she took it inside. We always wondered how she cooked it, because back in the village the belief was that a rabbit should never be eaten fresh. My mother smoked a rabbit over the fire for three days or dried it in the sun for long periods before cooking it in peanut butter sauce.

Miss Hutchinson never invited us to share the rabbit. We did not expect her to do so, because she was a white woman and white people did not easily mix with black people, let alone eat with them. This was Rhodesia, where the system of apartheid was similar to that practised in South Africa. But Miss Hutchinson was really not bad at all. Apart from calling us stupid Africans when she was very angry, she did actually love us. We did not mind being called stupid Africans, because Miss Hutchinson was kind and whenever she lost her temper she would apologise. After all, how many single women her age would have volunteered to leave beautiful England and come to a backward place like Kwenda Mission? Compared to stories of racist white people in the cities and on the farms, Miss Hutchinson was our saint.

Not long before independence, there were rumours that Miss Hutchinson was going back to England. She made a speech to the students in the school's big dining room. "Life has stages," she said. "My eight years in Africa are complete and it is time to leave. As you all grow up, you will finish school, find jobs, get married and move on to another stage." These words had an impact on me: I could see a ladder with different stages going up and up. The ladder was taking me somewhere far away from the village.

Two days later, we watched Miss Hutchinson's household goods being packed into a Methodist van. She shook hands with the African teachers and kissed the Mellor and McClure children. Then she took one last photograph of me and three other girls whose names I do not remember. I sat on the big rock behind the dormitories and watched the van disappear along the long, winding, dusty road towards the Wedza mountains. I could see the dust rising for miles behind the van. I tried to imagine how long it would take Miss Hutchinson to get to England. We were told that she would stay with some missionaries in Salisbury, then fly to South Africa. From there, she was going to fly to England. "England is the most beautiful place in the world. Civilised white people live there," my older brothers and sisters used to tell me. Watching the dust as the van with Miss Hutchinson in it left Kwenda Mission, I said that one day I would go away. I would start by following Miss Hutchinson to England, then go way beyond England to some faraway place. At the time, Australia did not exist in my mind.

Miss Hutchinson left her address with all the students. I was the first to write a letter to her. She wrote back to say that she had a photo of me smiling on her mantelpiece somewhere in Sheffield. "I miss Africa," she wrote. "I hope your people will not only continue to know the Lord, but will one day experience the freedom of political independence."

The liberation fighters came to Kwenda Mission soon after Miss Hutchinson left. The Mellors and the McClures were going to be killed but we begged for their lives, telling the freedom fighters that they were good white people. One night, all the white missionaries left and on the same night more than forty students disappeared into Mozambique for guerilla training. The next day I witnessed the torture and brutal harassment of local people who were suspected of having supported the freedom fighters. Both black and white soldiers physically assaulted teachers and senior students as well as our village elders. From then on, the war escalated in our area and young people of my age fled to the cities. The war paved the way for me to visit Harare for the first time.

After three years of training to be a nurse at the main hospital in Harare, I went to London to study for a diploma in child health. A few months later, I took the train to Sheffield. The Mellors and their two children met me at the station. Mrs Mellor shook my hand, but Mr Mellor gave me a bear hug and a kiss. He could never have done that in Zimbabwe. Their kids were now shy teenagers with freckles and they had completely forgotten the Shona language.

Dinner was pea-and-ham soup and homemade bread. I could not admit that I was hungry and would prefer something more filling. After dinner I announced that the next morning I planned to visit Miss Hutchinson. That was when the Mellors told me that Miss Hutchinson had peacefully died in her sleep three months before I arrived. She had died clutching the album that contained all her African photos.

"She was not discovered until three days later," Mrs Mellor said. She told me that Miss Hutchinson did not have a family; she was an adopted daughter, who'd been left behind when her

43

parents migrated to Australia in the 1940s. I was deeply upset by her death and also angry that no-one had been there to nurse her when she died. I felt that England had somehow let me down.

I still can't understand why I so badly wanted to see Miss Hutchinson. Perhaps I wanted her to see that I was no longer the bright smiling girl in her photo but an adult who could speak, laugh and even make jokes in her precious English language. And it would have been good if I had shared a meal with her at last. I also wanted to see the photo she had taken of me because I did not have any pictures of myself as a schoolgirl; perhaps I could reclaim my picture, now that she was gone.

I asked the Mellors whether they knew where Miss Hutchinson's personal property had been stored. They told me that most of it had been sold, but that her photo album had gone to the Methodist church library. I imagined my smiling photo tucked away in a huge box somewhere in cold, smoky Sheffield.

▰▰▰

Twenty years later, I am sitting on the same rock I sat on when Miss Hutchinson left. The dusty road which once wound its way past the African villages to the white men's farms has now been widened. I can see much more of the land out towards the mountains from my rock because most of the trees are gone.

An African couple with six children are living in Miss Hutchinson's house. The guttering system is no longer there, nor are the rabbits and the chickens. I ask Nelia, my fourteen-year-old niece, a boarder at the school, why the present teacher does not keep up the garden. She tells me that thieves broke in several times to steal not only the chickens and the rabbits, but the fences and the gardening tools as well.

It is Parents' Day at Kwenda Mission. I do not recall ever having Parents' Day when I was a student here; if we did have it, my parents never attended. I recognise faces among the parents because some of them were students here. They all tell me that standards have gone down. "Remember when Miss Hutchinson taught real agricultural science?" an old friend reminds me. The headmaster makes a speech and appeals for financial help towards the rebuilding of the school. Before the speech is over, I return to the rock near Miss Hutchinson's old house, where I just sit and think, trying to capture the past.

Looking away from what used to be the white men's farms, I focus on the area surrounding my village, thirty kilometres to the east. In the distance, I can see Dengedza, the mountain near where I was born. There were ten children in my family, two boys and eight girls. Except for Sydney and the three youngest girls, every one of us went to Kwenda Mission as a boarder. For four years we walked to school at the beginning of each term, carrying our books and our trunks. My father would sometimes deliver the trunks on his motorbike, which apart from the unreliable buses was the only vehicle in the area. We did not often use the bus because it was ten kilometres from our house to the bus stop and another two kilometres from the stop at the other end to the school. Moreover, bus fares for six children was something my parents could not afford.

Amai would prepare homemade peanut butter, roasted groundnuts, dried corn cobs and – if we were lucky – dried goat's meat for us to take to school. This would last us two or three weeks into term. After it ran out, we depended on our city friends being generous enough to share their jam, biscuits and sweets with us. As students from the villages, we were looked down on by our urban counterparts. On the first day of term, we arrived at school dirty, dusty, hungry and tired. But the few students from the city arrived in style by bus at sunset. In the dormitories, we watched these girls unpack their suitcases. For a couple of hours, they left items like chocolates, soft drinks, jam, bread, butter, tinned beef and other kinds of food on their beds for everyone to see. My sisters and I did not dare display our salted and sun-dried goat's meat.

I had one girlfriend from town who was very generous with what we called *zvechirungu*, or Western products. Patience's parents were Malawian migrants, domestic workers in Harare. She had access to the white madam's old clothes as well as receiving pocket money from her parents. But Patience could not get *zvechivanhu*, African things, like I did. So we swapped: a jar of jam for three cups of roasted groundnuts, a piece of sun-dried meat for two sweets. My friend would seal our trade agreement with a packet of soggy cold chips which we shared. I loved the smell of oil and vinegar. Patience would let me keep the empty brown paper packet so I could sniff the smell of civilisation. I told my sister Jessie that when I got a job one day, I would buy a dozen packets of chips with lots of oil and vinegar and eat them all. She laughed and said that by the time I had a salary, I would be interested in many other types of food.

Jessie was right. As I watch my niece unpack the parcel I have brought her, I certainly do not feel like eating a packet of cold chips – I feel like having a lovely cup of creamy, frothy cappuccino with no sugar. Before leaving Harare, I went to the supermarket and bought my niece all the kinds of food I wanted but could never get in boarding school. I also bought her toiletries, including tampons – luxuries I discovered when I was over twenty.

Nelia's joy and desire to show off to her friends cannot be

described. She wants to drag me along through all the dormitories, telling everyone that I am the aunt from Australia, the one she has always talked about. She points to Adam, who is busy explaining to one of the teachers how to heat water in a plastic container using solar technology. Nelia keeps calling Adam *murungu* or white man. She explains that Adam is not your average *murungu* because he loves spending time in the village. The young girls giggle and point to Adam, then turn away when he smiles at them. They ask Nelia why her aunt and her white partner have chosen to leave Australia and come to Zimbabwe. Why do they want to spend so much time in a boring village without running water or electricity? But Nelia avoids this question because she too does not understand why we make frequent visits to the village and even stay there for days at a time. I try to explain that for me, it is a kind of ambivalent homecoming, and that for Adam it is an interesting adventure.

When Adam and I drive away from the school, the students wave to us. I feel like Miss Hutchinson – except that I am not seventy, nor a white missionary. I want to convince myself that I am simply returning to my village and that nothing has changed. But a lot has: not only inside me, but in my family, in the village community and in the whole country.

▲▲▲

Baba died twenty-five years ago and his second wife has a new husband and four children. But people still talk about my father, remembering him as the founder of the first school in the area. They say he was a great man, because he managed to balance Christianity with traditional beliefs although it cost him his profession. I am not so convinced that Baba ever found a clear identity for himself between tradition and modernity. It is a precarious position, as his children know. Except for Sydney, all of us have left home; we live in Europe, the United States and Australia. For twenty years, we were never back in the village at the same time as a family until the day we buried Charles.

CHAPTER 4

Ngozi

HER NAME was Maria and she was my mother's distant niece. She was eighteen and blossoming into a beautiful young woman, but already people were speaking of her as an old maid in the making.

The young men in her village were all afraid of her. They said Maria was possessed by a spirit of a man long dead. At times she would descend into a trancelike state: her face would darken and her voice would become low and gruff, rumbling out from her as if from the depths of the earth. Her suitors would take flight at these times, fearing for their lives.

Maria would often disappear off into the hills where she would spend the day wandering around the forests and talking to herself. At home she would sit under a tree and refuse to speak to anyone, except to the voice that she said was communicating with her secretly.

Her parents and grandparents tried hard to find a solution to what they called her 'strange madness' but had no success. Then her grandparents suggested that they take her to a *n'anga*. After consulting his spirit advisers, the *n'anga* said that Maria was possessed by a *ngozi* spirit which desired to make itself known.

A *ngozi* could only reveal itself at a special ceremony held in his or her honour. In the days before white man's law, it was a *ngozi* who would impose justice in the village, demanding compensation for wrongdoings; nobody would ever defy the word of a *ngozi*. The problem was that this *ngozi* was reluctant to reveal itself, seeming to enjoying its new home in Maria's mind.

As Maria became more womanly, so the *ngozi* grew, as if the two were connected. At first the words she spoke in her trances had been unintelligible, but over time the trances were becoming more frequent and public, and her speech was becoming more distinct. The old people began talking about drought and disease, and wondered whose family the calamity would befall. A reckoning for matters long forgotten was on the way.

▰▲▲▰

One day I arrived at the homestead and found Amai busy preparing to visit her maiden village.

"There is going to be a big ceremony for Maria in my village," she told me. "Would you mind driving me over there tomorrow?"

My mother was lucky that I had arrived that Friday evening because there was no direct transport to her village. Since 1948, she had had to walk between her village and my father's. It was forty-five dusty kilometres by the road, but she would go cross-country, threading her way through the thick forest, occasionally climbing high enough to see the spectacular views of this high plateau. But Amai had no time for the scenery. She walked with a slight stoop, looking down and singing old hymns to herself as she quietly went her way.

She would normally set out in the dark, after the first cock crew, and by dawn she would be crossing the Rwenje River, leaving her footprints in its sandy banks even before the hordes of children who crossed there on their way to school. She would arrive at her destination just before lunch time.

As children, we dreaded accompanying Amai to her village. But there were some rewards to the journey: we could stop halfway and sit in the shade, and my mother would then give us delicious cold chicken and rice. This was a special dish which we usually only got at Easter time or on Christmas day or when a favourite relative came to visit.

Amai, Sydney and I left on Saturday afternoon. Sydney enjoyed the drive: he urged me to stop at three shopping centres where he restocked his beer supply and told everyone he met what a wonderful sister I was. Amai sat in the back, imperiously ignoring her friends as we passed their huts in a blur of dust and smoke from cooking fires.

The journey that used to take part of the night and all the morning took less than forty-five minutes in an air-conditioned four-wheel drive. When we arrived, my mother's extended family of many nieces, nephews, cousins and sisters-in-law greeted us with great joy. I had met most of the women who had married into Amai's family at Charles's funeral. As usual, about ten of them were busy working – cooking, carrying water or brewing *doro*. The older women sat on the verandah of their huts, drinking the warm, home-brewed sorghum beer. Several children, some of them half-naked, played in the sand. Several men sat around on logs, smoking and drinking beer some distance from the women. An old man was warming a drum as the sun slipped behind the hills. He turned the skin slowly in front of the fire, drumming softly now and again, making a noise like a far-off storm.

After the evening meal, the elders gathered in my uncle's big hut and the singing and dancing started. For quite some time, Maria just sat among the other women, talking and laughing with them. I was rather puzzled by her apparently normal behaviour. I asked Amai how and when Maria was going to be possessed. How would people know the *ngozi* was present?

"You wait and see. It may take all night before the spirit reveals itself." I realised that occasions like these needed patience.

The songs continued and the women danced. Some time after midnight, Maria slowly, almost mechanically, joined the women who were dancing. The more she danced, the more people sang and the louder the drum was pounded. I think it was about an hour later that I heard Maria's voice rise above everyone else's – it was no longer the voice of a young woman but that of a man.

Someone placed a stool on the dance floor and everyone sat around it in complete silence. The fire was low and the night sounds of the forest had all but died away. Maria went outside briefly, then walked back in and sat on the stool. Men clapped and women ululated.

"We welcome you, stranger," said one of my oldest uncles.

"I am not a stranger to this village," said the voice inside Maria.

By now all the older people had no trouble recognising the voice. "We are aware of that," my uncle replied. "Please do not be angry with us. We know that you have been to our village before. But we know so little about you. What is your name?"

"Cigarette, please," the voice said. Someone gave Maria a cigarette and a box of matches. She lit up and drew quietly on the cigarette, her eyes moving furtively from one face to another as if looking for somebody in particular. For a good while she stared at the women, then turned away abruptly and started to sob, almost with relief.

"I did not do any harm to you," said the voice. "My name is Chiutsi. Before the war I frequently visited this village. I had some business to do with some of you people."

"We know," said my uncles and clapped their hands.

"Then you let me be killed here. I had done nothing wrong."

"We know. But it was not our fault," said my oldest uncle. "You were responsible for your own murder."

"But you could have spared my life. How could you allow a stranger to die among your people? I do not belong to your totem. You should have protected me," said Chiutsi.

By now Maria had left the scene completely, and had been replaced by a middle-aged man with sharp glittering eyes and tousled hair. He jabbed the air with his fingers accusingly as he spoke to the elders. There were lines of phosphorescence streaming like fireflies from his limbs.

"We had no choice," my uncle replied. "But why are you here now? Why are you taking our daughter?"

"Because I deserved a respectable death and a better burial. I need some compensation. If you do not do that, you know what the consequences are."

"As you say," said my uncle. "But tell us what to do. We know that our village must be cleansed. How shall we do it?"

"The girl must go. She is my wife," Chiutsi declared, glaring out as if expecting to be challenged.

"Give us some time," said one of the men.

"You have had plenty of time. I died seventeen years ago. My wife is ready for me now. How much more time do you want?" Chiutsi lit another cigarette.

"As you say," my uncle replied.

"I want to go now. If I do not get what is due to me, I shall return."

"We have heard you," Amai said and started ululating. Maria began shaking vigorously and coughing.

"Chiutsi is leaving," my mother whispered to me. Within a few minutes, Maria had returned and appeared normal again. She asked for some water, then quietly left to go to bed.

"She does not even know that she was under spirit possession," Amai said as we went outside with a few of the women for some fresh air.

"Who was Chiutsi?" I asked.

My mother's sister started telling me the story. "We never knew where he came from but we knew that he owned the small grocery nearby. Before the war, he used to come to this village selling fish on his bicycle. Then he fell in love with Maria's mother, Anne. As you know, Zachea, her husband, worked in the mines in South Africa for many years. People warned Anne that she was committing adultery. Although she did not conduct the affair openly, everyone, including her children, knew about her relationship with Chiutsi. Zachea's brothers then warned Chiutsi that if he kept on seeing Anne, they would kill him. Chiutsi took no notice.

"One night the guerillas came to the village and called a meeting. They talked about their suffering in many parts of the world, and then said that certain traitors cared little about the sacrifices the freedom fighters were making.

" 'Are there any traitors among you?' their leader asked.

" 'Yes, I know of a traitor,' said one of Zachea's brothers. 'Come, I will show you where he is.'

"That very night Chiutsi had been seen going into Anne's bedroom. We all watched, as he was dragged half-naked out of her hut and forced to sit in the midst of the crowd.

" 'Is this the sell-out?' the freedom fighter asked.

" 'Yes,' answered Zachea's brother.

" 'Where did you find him?' the freedom fighter asked.

" 'He was making love to my brother's wife.'

"The guerillas laughed. 'What a real patriot this man is,' the leader said. 'Imagine making love to another man's wife while we are busy fighting for his independence. And where is the prostitute who dares to insult her husband so publicly? Let her identify herself.'

"Anne was pushed into the centre of the crowd, her baby, Maria, snuggled in her arms. She too was half-naked and shivering.

" 'Is this what you want to see in a new Zimbabwe?' the freedom fighter asked. No-one said anything.

" 'Answer me!' he roared.

" 'No,' we replied.

"Just then a young man from across the river arrived at a run. 'There are some soldiers camping behind the hill,' he panted.

" 'Disperse!' shouted the leader of the guerillas.

"The crowd quickly broke up. I do not know exactly what happened then but some people say that the freedom fighter shot Chiutsi in the stomach and he fell down and bled to death. Anne was given a blow to the head and she fell down unconscious, still holding the baby.

"The following morning, Zachea's brothers carried Anne to her maiden village where she later recovered. Chiutsi's body lay out in the sun all day until evening. Then some men took the body and buried it in a shallow grave between two large rocks. For five years, Anne did not return to the village. Then her husband returned and brought her back here. He built her a beautiful house and paid little attention to the stories about Chiutsi. But it would be naive to believe that Chiutsi was gone forever. Members of his clan knew that his body was still here. It was only a question of time before he revealed himself."

I had listened quietly. But it all seemed so unfair to everyone involved. The people in the village had not killed Chiutsi, so it seemed cruel that his spirit should demand compensation from them.

"That is the way it is," my aunt explained, when I voiced my thoughts. "If a stranger dies in your village and he is not buried properly, he has the right to demand compensation from the people."

"But why take Maria? She had nothing to do with a love affair between her mother and Chiutsi," I said.

"That is just the way it is," said my aunt.

"What is to be done next?" I asked.

"Your uncles will now search for Chiutsi's relatives and present Maria to them. A male member of his family will then take Maria as his wife. She will live with Chiutsi's family for the rest of her life and bear children with Chiutsi's name."

"What if Maria does not want to do this?" I asked.

"She has no choice," my aunt replied and went back into the hut.

The following morning life seemed to be going on as normal. While a few women were preparing big pots of tea, I asked Maria whether she would like to accompany me to the river for a bath. She happily agreed. "In fact, I was hoping to have a chat with you before you leave today," she said.

Carrying a small bucket and my toilet bag, I followed her to the river. I wanted to ask her about the previous night's events but I did not know how to begin. Maria sang a little tune as she walked. When we got to the bathing hole she put down her empty clay water pot, took my bucket and started washing her feet and scrubbing them gently with a stone.

"Maria," I said, looking away, "people are saying that you are possessed by the spirit of a dead man. They say that you will bring bad times to the village. Are you possessed?"

"I do not think so. In fact, I do not believe in spirit possession."

"But I thought the whole ceremony last night was done so that the spirit which possesses you will come out and identify itself."

"I know. But it didn't, did it?" she asked anxiously, looking at me.

"I am not sure," I said. Was she just playing a game with me? Surely she must know what had happened.

"The truth is, sometimes I believe in spirit possession and sometimes I do not," she confessed, softly.

"Do you know how the spirit came to live in your body?" I asked.

"Last night people told me that when Chiutsi was murdered and my mother was assaulted, I was left on the ground with the two bodies as everyone else had fled from the government soldiers. And there I lay between my mother and her dying lover. Everybody was worried that I had been with the dead man and would suffer from *ngozi*, particularly since the man had died as he had. People have always treated me differently, as if they wanted the *ngozi* to come to me, to free them from their guilt. When I was growing up, they always asked me whether Chiutsi had come and finally I started to hear him. Every now and again, I hear him saying, 'Why did you kill me? Bury me among my people.' My mother tells me to ignore these voices but I can't. But if I am mad it is the fault of the villagers."

"Do you believe that you were possessed last night?" I asked.

"Maybe, maybe not. I speak like Chiutsi all the time, so if they say I was possessed, it does not surprise me."

I felt so sorry for Maria. Even as we talked, arrangements for her 'marriage' into Chiutsi's family were under way. She was not allowed to participate in a decision that would affect her for the rest of her life. I wanted to help her, but how was I going to do that? Then an idea struck me.

"I may be able to get you a job as a housemaid in Harare," I said.

Maria's face lit up. She stood up and performed a little dance. "I will be so glad if you can do that for me. You will be my saviour," she said. "When will you know if there is a job available?"

"As soon as I get to Harare, I will call my sister and ask if she still requires a housemaid. Then I will send you a letter by bus next Wednesday if the job is available. I will do my best," I promised.

She shook my hand and got dressed. In silence, we fetched water and walked back to the village.

After lunch, as we prepared to leave, Maria shook my hand again and whispered, "Do not forget. I have to get away." I nodded and drove off.

"A *ngozi* wife can never live with anyone except her husband's people. You will be wasting your time getting Maria a job," Amai told me on the way home.

As it turned out, I could not find Maria a job immediately. And before long, word passed back to me that she had followed the custom and had been taken as a *ngozi* wife. First, two men from her family had paid a formal visit to Makumbe, where Chiutsi came from. They announced to his immediate family that Chiutsi's restless body was still on their land and admitted their guilt for killing him. Chiutsi's family complained that Maria's family had taken too long to compensate them. After several apologies were made and fines paid, Chiutsi's family arranged reburial for their son. Shortly afterwards, Maria was taken by two of her father's sisters to her 'husband's' family. She had become a full *ngozi* wife.

"Unfair. Totally unfair on the women," Sydney said. "Would you let that happen to your daughter?" he asked Amai.

"No."

"So why do you let it happen to your niece?"

"It is a custom. *Ngozi* demands compensation and a young virgin has to pay," she replied.

"Sometimes customs are evil and oppressive. Do you agree?"

"I do."

"But it is you, the senior women of the village, who are participating in this practice. The men who betrayed Chiutsi are still at large – marrying more wives and happily drinking beer. And Maria has to pay for their crime. It is just not fair. We must change these traditions. Don't you think so?" He turned to me.

"I fully agree," I said.

▰▰▰

A few weeks later, I met one of my mother's nephews from her maiden village and I asked him about Maria. "When the decision to take her to her husband's family was made, she did not protest," he said. "She went to Chiutsi's mother's house and lived there for three days. On the second day, two of his brothers and three male cousins came to claim her on the grounds that any of them could be her husband. This was really hard for Maria. Imagine having to sleep with these men she didn't know. So on the third day she ran away."

Two months went by and I assumed Maria had settled back in her own village, so I was surprised to hear that she had returned to Chiutsi's village of her own accord. Chiutsi's brothers and cousins were understandably overjoyed to see her return. They had never got on with their prosperous brother, who had always accused them of trying to steal his money, and here he was, from the grave as it were, providing them with a beautiful new wife who would bear their children and work in the fields. How fortunate that such customs had not died away, they said as they celebrated with quarts of store-bought beer.

Maria was given her own hut near the hopeful bridegrooms. But she had other ideas. Whenever one of the men would come to her hut at night, she would belittle their manhood in a loud, deep voice, saying that they were just shadows of Chiutsi. She called them grave robbers and accused them of using the customs to their own advantage. In the darkness, Maria's words boomed out so the whole village could hear and the men ran back to their wives in shame. Once one of them tried to force himself upon Maria, but she threw him off easily, as if he were a child, and chased him away with a burning branch from the fire.

The men left her alone after that, convinced that she had again been possessed by another malevolent spirit. But the old women of the village knew the truth: the spirit of Chiutsi had settled within the girl and would never leave. The men were taking advantage of the custom for their own ends and *ngozi* would never let that happen. So jealous was Chiutsi of Maria that he would never let another man take her for a wife, not even one of his own brothers.

The last time I saw Maria, she was paying a visit to her mother. She was walking in the barren hills near the village and I watched her from a distance. She had grown even more beautiful and remote. She strolled along with no particular purpose, occasionally singing a little song or talking to herself – a solitary figure who was never alone.

CHAPTER 5

Sunday Morning in the Village...

IT IS SUNDAY, and a warm winter's day. We are in the month of June; it gets quite cold in the morning and in the evening, but the afternoons are mild and beautiful. Except for the doves and an occasional cow mooing, it's extremely quiet; life moves at a very slow pace here in the village.

I wake up at dawn and watch the sun rise over the hills. For years, Amai has regretted building the homestead on the foothills because the shade from the hills means that we get the sunshine a little later than our neighbours across the valley. I watch the rays shine through the few tall trees left on the hillside, yawn widely and wonder whether anyone has been thoughtful enough to light the fire in the kitchen.

"How about a cup of tea?" Adam asks. I want to ask him to go and make it himself. But I know that he could not: gathering firewood and making a fire would take him ages, and in any case, according to tradition, my mother would not allow him to do it.

"Tea will be ready in half an hour," I tell him.

"We should have a small gas ring, so that when we want a cup of tea we can just make it without going through all that rigmarole of gathering firewood and fetching water," he says. "Life shouldn't be this difficult."

"It is not that hard. Lighting a fire is no big deal."

But when I go down to the kitchen, I find that the fireplace is full of last night's ashes. "No fire yet?" I ask Sis Anna. "Where is Amai?"

"She has gone to look for a goat that did not come home last night."

"Will you light the fire for me, please?"

Sis Anna helps my mother around the homestead. She is about twenty years old and has lived with my mother for six months. Since we have all left home, my mother needs domestic help as well as company. If these were the old days, she would have been looking after several grandchildren; once a child got off the breast, he was taken to his grandmother so that a new sibling could enjoy the mother's nurturing. But these days people living in the city simply take their children to crèche or kindergarten, leaving village grandmothers stripped of their former roles.

Sis Anna is likely to stay with my mother until she finds a young man to marry her. She is paid one hundred and fifty dollars a month, a fair salary for a village housemaid. In the city she would be earning the same or a little bit more, but here she has no expenses so she can save money. She does all the work that is required around the homestead, which includes all the house-work, working in the field and, occasionally, caring for Sydney's youngest two children when my sister-in-law is not at home. When my mother goes to the city, Sis Anna looks after the household and also cooks for Simba, the herd boy, and Mr Christmas, the handyman.

Simba came to live with my mother when he was fifteen. He passed Grade Six but then his parents couldn't afford to send him to school. His responsibilities are mainly to do with the cattle, goats, dogs and chickens. During the rainy season, he wakes up at sunrise, yokes the oxen and ploughs Amai's field. Later he might milk the cows or take the herd for grazing until sunset. His salary is about the same as Sis Anna's but Simba has more privileges that Sis Anna because he has been with my mother for four years. He is like my mother's youngest son – she buys clothes for him and gets worried when he is late coming home.

Sometimes I think Simba is getting too old to herd cattle. He has taken to hanging around the small shopping centre near our homestead when he is not working, an oversized cassette player glued to his ear. There is nothing flash about this little centre, which is just a couple of shops on a bend in the road. They sell razor blades and floor wax, warm beer and ancient sweets. But for Simba, this is the extent of society; he puts on his best clothes and charges the batteries for his radio in the sun for the occasion. Some days there are no other people there at all, so he just sits with the old shopkeeper, waiting for customers. Simba has never been to Harare, never seen television or eaten a McDonald's hamburger, but he seems none the worse for wear and has shown no interest in visiting the city.

I have known Christmas, who is in his late fifties or early sixties, since I was a child. He was the village drummer, and was known as Christmas because he was born on some long-forgotten Christmas day. He still wears an ancient overcoat, a pair of pants that is a patchwork of stains and mendings, and sandals made from old tyres tied with strips of hide. You never see him without a cigarette rolled from newspaper and home-grown tobacco at the corner of his mouth.

He used to live down the valley with his wife and children. Then one year his pregnant wife went back to her parents to deliver their fifth child and did not come back. The story told was that Mrs Christmas was in labour for three days and her enlarged thyroid got bigger and bigger. The baby died on delivery and soon after Mrs Christmas died too; that must have been twenty years ago.

Over the years that followed, Christmas played the drum at village parties, had a long-term affair with a widow, worked as a security guard for a shopkeeper and did various handyman jobs for my mother in exchange for the odd pair of trousers or a T-shirt. When the shopkeeper no longer needed him, Christmas found himself spending a lot of time at our homestead. Sydney asked him to do all the manly duties such as cutting firewood or repairing the garden fence; gradually, Christmas started staying the night, sleeping in Simba's room.

Simba resented his presence and a conflict arose. Then my sister-in-law offered Christmas formal employment as the homestead gardener and handyman at sixty dollars per month, with accommodation, food and beer provided. Christmas gladly accepted his new position and with it his own room, away from Simba.

▰▰▰

Adam sits on the verandah reading Australian newspapers that are three weeks old. Jack and his five-year-old cousin Ruvimbo are busy chasing chickens and goats or drawing pictures in the dust. Sydney, who is slowly recovering from last night's beer, sits on a log next to Amai and her older sister, Maiguru (big mother), who is staying with us for a few days. Maiguru is busy shelling groundnuts. Taking a smooth stone, my mother grinds the oily nuts against a large flat rock until a peanut butter paste slowly oozes off into a tin.

Christmas is smoking his cigarette and drinking *chandada*, the lethal, twenty-four-hour home-brew which is concocted from sorghum, corn meal, yeast and sugar. Three skinny dogs skulk around the fringes of the courtyard hoping for some fresh peanut butter. Christmas deftly aims an empty bottle at the boldest dog. It misses and skitters off the dust into the house, breaking in the living room. Sis Anna drags herself to her feet to clear up the shards of glass.

People passing by stop at the homestead gate and shout greetings.

"How is everyone's health?" one woman calls.

"We are all well. Good morning," my mother shouts back. She can identify most villagers by their voices.

If the passer-by is a close relative or friend, he shouts, "Good morning. Are the children and the grandchildren all in good health?"

"Yes, they are. Will you please come in and have something to eat?"

"No, thank you. We will eat another day." And whoever it is moves on.

Even late at night, people call out the greetings. In the past, it was common for strangers to stop by and shout the greetings. When my mother could not identify the voice, she used to call back, "I do not recognise the voice. Who is it?"

"You will not be able to tell who we are. We are strangers to this part of the country."

"So where are you going at night?"

If the strangers were going far, they often replied, "The sun has gone down on us." This meant that they wanted to stay the night.

If Amai felt that they were good people, she would invite them into the house and cook for them; only after eating would she enquire after their totem and their people. In the discussions which followed, it always ended up that our family was related to that of the strangers. For example, if the stranger's totem was antelope, he was my father's brother because my father's totem is antelope; if he was a buffalo, then he was my mother's brother because my mother's totem is buffalo. Sometimes totems could be very distant – but in the end my mother would say, "Ah, but my sister is married to the people of the monkey totem, so you are my brother-in-law."

In the morning, the strangers, now regarded as relatives, were fed and bidden farewell.

Those were the old days. People do not make overnight journeys any more, now that the bus passes the villages twice a day. When the bus breaks down, as it does frequently, the passengers will stay with it until it is fixed, even if it takes days. People are losing the memory of the freedom that walking down these dusty roads brings.

Since it is unlikely that a total stranger will pass by these days and ask to stay the night, Amai is even less likely to miss an opportunity to show hospitality to visitors. She knows all the people in the villages around. Our homestead is like a drop-in centre on Sundays, as we are on the main track used by people travelling between villages and herd boys taking their cattle to the river for grazing. Some people are on their way to the church, a beer party or to visit a relative a few kilometres past our homestead; others just come and sit around for a few hours, and then go home. Amai welcomes them all. She cooks for close friends and offers sweet tea or cordial to acquaintances. But if there is some home-brewed beer, everyone sits around and drinks from the same cup. Sometimes the group will simply sit drinking in silence, as there is no need for frivolous chat if there is nothing important to say.

Our first guest today is Mai Hilda from up the hill. I have known Mai Hilda since I was a child; in fact, she was one of the traditional mid-wives who delivered me in a small hut down near the river. She is one of my mother's close friends. She has a pretty, round face, brown-stained teeth, and a big bosom that swims inside an old Pepsi T-shirt. Her little, short feet have large cracks and she wears sandals made from car tyres.

"Welcome," Mai Hilda says and shakes my hand. "When did you arrive?"

"Last night," I reply sitting on a mat next to her.

After five minutes or so, I clap my hands in the traditional way expected of women and ask about Mai Hilda's health, calling her by her husband's totem. Failing to clap hands and to ask about someone's health is regarded by the elders as totally disrespectful. It also means that you have become so Westernised that you do not think village customs are important.

"I am very well, except for frequent headaches. Did you bring any tablets for me?"

"No. Not this time." Village people always ask for pills to cure minor ailments. There is a belief that even one antibiotic will do miracles for a headache. My mother keeps a small First Aid box and when someone gets desperate, she offers them the occasional Panadol or Aspirin, or Betadine spray for a wound.

"Where is the beer party today?" Mai Hilda asks Christmas, who has stopped drinking *chandada*. The container is nowhere to be seen. Christmas is well known for hiding his beer when neighbours arrive unexpectedly.

"No beer today unless you go down to Mai Jane's place," says Christmas, trying to conceal the glow that comes from drinking *chandada* in the morning.

"I will see how I feel in a little while. Do you want to come with me if I decide to go?" Mai Hilda asks my mother.

"No, I do not like *chandada*. It gives me a headache," Amai replies. "Stay and help me grind this peanut butter. My back is beginning to hurt from the constant movement."

"Your back is old now. Why not let this young back do it for you?" Mai Hilda points at me.

But they all know that I cannot grind peanut butter. In fact, I was never regarded as a hard-working young girl when it came to back-breaking village chores, where a simple task can take up a whole day. For years I longed to escape this kind of work and now I feel a sense of relief whenever I watch village women engaged in their daily routines – I am glad to be just an observer and no longer a participant. The idea of working so hard for so little fills me with horror. I admire these women's resilience and determination, but deep down inside me I know that I am no longer part of their world.

Mai Hilda's story is typical of the women of my mother's generation. Her parents were very poor, so they offered her to an older man, Makwanya, as a second wife, when she was no more than fourteen or fifteen years old. Makwanya already had ten grown-up children and several grandchildren. But his first wife and his own children did not want to be near him because he was rumoured to have tuberculosis.

One day, Amai and Mai Hilda went out mushroom-gathering before sunrise and Makwanya was asked to look after us children. He did not have to do anything except check that none of us fell into the fire smouldering outside, where he sat all day warming himself. He wore a big coat and coughed and coughed incessantly, often spitting horrible yellow phlegm into the ashes.

I played near him for a while and listened to his cough; when he fell asleep very close to the fire, I ran away to play in the house with my sisters. When Mai Hilda and Amai returned, we heard loud wailing: they shouted that Makwanya was dead. All the villagers arrived and a mourning ritual started. I had been the last person to see him alive; whenever I saw his ghost passing by after dark, I would wish it goodnight.

So Mai Hilda became a widow when she was barely seventeen. Her father wanted her back in his village, but Mai Hilda met Chigondo, a widower with three children, and married him. After Mai Hilda had three miscarriages, her sister sent her own two-year-old daughter, Hilda, to keep Mai Hilda company and spare her the shame of not being called by a child's name.

I once asked Amai whether Mai Hilda had ever had a child of her own.

"Yes, she did," my mother replied. "Her fifth pregnancy went as far as eight months. She boarded the bus to the district hospital and we did not see her for two weeks. Then one evening she returned: I remember it so vividly. I was in the courtyard when I saw her walking slowly towards my house with a baby on her back. I rushed to embrace and congratulate her, but I quickly changed my mind because the look of sadness on her face was unbearable. We shook hands and walked silently into my hut, and then she started sobbing hysterically. The baby on her back was dead.

"After she had calmed down, I took the baby away from her, placed it on a mat and shrouded it in two blankets. Mai Hilda said the baby had been alive when he was born prematurely. He lived for three days and then died. As soon as she was told that her baby was dead, Mai Hilda strapped the little body onto her back and sneaked out of the hospital before anyone could stop her. In those days it was impossible to carry a corpse on any form of public transport. The nurses at the hospital would tell you that your baby was dead and if you did not have private transport to take it to the village, they simply incinerated it. There was no ceremony and there could never be a grave for your child. This is the reason why most women preferred to give birth at home.

"Mai Hilda said she wanted to show her husband and his relatives that she had been woman enough to deserve the title of mother. So she spent the whole day on the bus with the dead baby carefully held on her lap; she even pretended to breast-feed it so that no-one would become suspicious.

"That was Mai Hilda's last pregnancy; she did not try again. But from time to time she still goes down to the valley and stands by her baby's grave."

"I have some nice sun-dried mushrooms for you." Mai Hilda's voice brings me back to the present. "Drop in tomorrow morning and I will have them ready." She washes her hands and takes over the grinding. Amai happily moves away and starts to help Maiguru with patchworking a brown quilt.

A few minutes later, Jaison, a man from another village, stops by. He is the hut-thatcher, painter, bricklayer and carpenter in all the villages around. Last year, he started re-painting Amai's house but left the job unfinished because he had to attend to a sick cousin. Having spent all the money Amai paid him, he is back to ask when he can begin painting again.

Jaison is married to my childhood best friend, Beatrice. Today he has the dishevelled look of a man who has not been spending much time at home lately. His eyes keep darting around as if he is expecting an attack from an enemy – most probably Beatrice. He is a tall, well-built man who would be handsome were it not for the pronounced dent over his left eyebrow, the legacy of a battle with his wife. Having come home drunk one evening, he hit Beatrice for failing to have his dinner ready and then slumped down by the fire where he dozed. He awoke to the terrible sight of Beatrice looming over him with an axe raised high. Screaming vengeance, she plunged her weapon down, but managed only a glancing blow to the side of her husband's head as he rolled away. Jaison recovered – Beatrice nursed him with great remorse – but his eye bulged out monstrously from its shattered socket whenever he laughed or had too much to drink.

From the conversation, I gather that Beatrice now has an eye injury of her own.

"How is Beatrice?" Mai Hilda asks.

"Much better. She was lucky because the stone hit her just above the eyebrow."

"You could have killed her if the ancestral spirits had not intervened," says Amai.

"What happened?" I ask.

"It was an eye for an eye," says Jaison, his damaged face twisting into a horrible leer. He laughs the way heroes do before they boast how they conquered an enemy. "Oh that day, people! About that day I will have to say one thing – I learnt that one man on his own should never attempt to thrash his wife in the presence of other women. When I hit my wife with a stone, it was a last resort to protect myself."

"Do not defend yourself before you tell us the story," Mai Hilda interrupts.

"What happened was very simple," continues Jaison. "It was like this. My wife and I were invited to my cousin's wedding. There was so much alcohol. As you all know, my wife drinks beer. Nothing wrong in a woman drinking, do not get me wrong. She can drink all she wants as long as she remains respectful and maintains decency. She should also not forget her usual duties such as caring for her children. But on that day, my wife drank so much that by late afternoon alcohol had defeated her. She disappeared and I did not know where she was.

"Our youngest baby was eight months old and still on the breast. The baby was seen by people crawling in the sand in search of its mother. I took the baby and nursed it while I looked for my wife. After searching everywhere, I found her asleep on a mattress in one of the guest rooms. Nothing wrong with that, except that this was the room where the bride's father was also sleeping. But do not get me wrong, they were not sleeping in the same bed – he was on the bed while she was on the floor. I put the baby onto the breast and then woke up my wife. She managed to get up and left to walk home.

"I continued enjoying the party as if nothing had happened. But soon after sunset, I went home too. I asked my wife why she had neglected the baby and why she had chosen to sleep in the same room as the father of the bride. Do you know what her reply was?"

"No," we all chorus.

"She said that she had every right to lie down wherever she wished. We started arguing loudly. You know I have three young brothers, don't you? Well, their wives heard the argument and they came to try and reconcile my wife and me. They all agreed that my wife had done the wrong thing. But did my wife listen? No. Instead, she told me that I was a useless, skinny husband. I got angry and slapped her twice, very hard. Just to teach her a lesson. But when I started punching her, the three women grabbed some burning pieces of firewood and started chasing me. I then realised that in my pocket I had a catapult that I use for hitting birds. I stopped running and shouted that they should all disperse or I was going to hit them. All the women fled, except for my wife. She challenged me to hit her. I paused and then aimed the catapult directly at her head. The stone hit her hard and she fell. Her legs twitched in the air.

"The other women rushed back to my wife and I did too. There was a deep cut just above her eye and blood everywhere. A message was quickly sent to her parents and her father arrived that same night. Fortunately, by the time he arrived, Beatrice had regained consciousness.

"No-one discussed what had happened until the next morning, when I was summoned to a village hearing. I explained that my wife had humiliated my manhood by not caring for my daughter and by sleeping in the same room with another man. My father-in-law agreed that my wife was wrong and so did all the other men. The village headman warned me not to use a catapult again and ordered me to take Beatrice to the health centre. That was how I nearly killed her and she very well deserved it."

"But surely you should not assault your wife for such a small offence. You could be charged by the police for such violence," I say.

"It was an offence to my dignity," Jaison says, going back into the kitchen to light another cigarette. When he returns, he pauses in the doorway: "If I had gone to jail for assault, I would have come back after six months or more of hard labour to kick her out of my house for a few months."

Everyone shakes their heads in disbelief. Christmas whispers, "It is not his house – it belongs to Beatrice. He contributes nothing to it. No wonder she finds other ways of generating income."

I am about to ask what he means when Mai Hilda signals to me to keep quiet.

"If there is no beer around here, I better be on my way," Jaison says. We wish him a good day and he leaves.

When he is out of earshot, Mai Hilda starts laughing. "Fancy calling himself a man. If he hadn't used the catapult, Beatrice would have beaten him to nothing! That woman is something else."

"She certainly is," Christmas agrees. "But I think she overdoes this whoring around. Imagine making love to the father of the bride so openly."

"But Jaison said they were sleeping in separate places – not on the same bed," I protest.

They all laugh. "Do not be so naive," Mai Hilda says. "Have you ever heard of a man who admits that he found another man on top of his wife? The truth is, the father of the bride and Beatrice were caught in action. But Jaison cannot bring himself to say this openly. In fact when Beatrice recovered from the injury, she pointed out that he had made a big deal out of something which could have been kept private. She also said that he had given her the licence to find more short-term lovers.

"Jaison knows about Beatrice's affairs but he no longer seems to care. He even defends his wife against other people's criticisms. Beatrice manages to send their children to boarding school through her own efforts as both a whore and a farmer. Do you know that last year she sold the highest number of maize bags to the Grain Marketing Board?"

"Such a hard worker – she deserves a better man," Amai remarks. She turns to Sis Anna, who is washing dishes nearby. "Sis Anna, it is time to start thinking about lunch."

No matter whether it is lunch or dinner, we always have *sadza*, or maize meal porridge, for the basic main dish. So when my mother plans meals, she thinks in terms of which vegetables are

75

going to accompany the *sadza*. Meat is a luxury down here. When we were children we looked forward to close relatives visiting us, as a chicken or a goat would be slaughtered for the occasion.

Sometimes my father would kill a larger animal for us during school holidays. The saddest part about the killing of a bull or a cow was when we saw the butchers, two of our neighbours, arrive with their sharp knives and axes. They would tie the poor beast to a tree and lay fresh branches alongside for the carcass to fall on. Amai always made sure that we were safely locked in one of the bedrooms before the first stroke landed on the beast's neck. But she could not stop us from hearing the excruciating sounds the animal made as it received blow after blow. Gradually, these noises would get fainter and fainter until there was a loud thud and we knew that the killing was done. We would bang on the door and Amai would let us out. One by one, we would run out to watch what happened next.

The butchers were rewarded with a saucepanful of blood each, a piece of liver, and a piece of the breast if the animal was a cow or the testicles if it was a bull. After skinning the carcass, they would boil up the blood with their bits of meat and then relax to eat their special dish. Baba often gave them an extra chunk of meat each to take home so they could share it with their wives and children.

For the rest of those school holidays, we would eat cooked, sun-dried beef with our *sadza* every day. But if a cow or bull wasn't slaughtered, as sometimes happened, we had to be satisfied with a few meals of goat meat or simply fresh or dried vegetables for the whole of our holidays.

Very little has changed. For most village people, it is a struggle to get fresh vegetables, let alone a small piece of meat to eat with their *sadza*. My mother is considered lucky because whenever one of my sisters comes back to the village from overseas, her hand luggage contains at least ten kilos of tinned food: sardines, pilchards in tomato sauce, anchovies and baked quails for Amai's *sadza*. And Rudo and I regularly make a trip to the abattoirs in Harare where we buy meat in bulk, which we dry in the sun in my back yard and store in big bags to bring to Amai. So whenever she cooks *sadza* in the village, my mother eats it with a small piece of meat or some tinned fish. But when there are neighbours around, she pretends to be just as desperate as everyone else for something other than vegetables. Only when she is absolutely positive that no-one from the village will be joining her for a meal does she open a tin of sardines. This Sunday is one of those days when she is crying poor.

"Sis Anna, do check if we still have any dried pumpkin leaves in the granary." Sis Anna goes to the granary and brings back some unattractive grey leaves. Amai tells her to prepare them for lunch.

"Those pumpkin leaves are very nice if you add tomatoes and peanut butter," says Christmas.

"True. But I prefer fresh pumpkin leaves to dried ones," Maiguru says.

"If I eat any more dried vegetables I will die!" exclaims Sydney.

"You are a school-teacher – you should be able to buy meat more often," says Maiguru.

"He spends all his money on alcohol," says Christmas. "Didn't you hear him singing last night after yet another Saturday of drinking?"

"He always sings when he comes home drunk," Amai says.

"But why do you do that? Why do you want to wake everyone

up?" Maiguru asks.

"I do not remember that I sang last night. If I did, I meant to scare away the ghosts," Sydney laughs. "The *doro* I drank yesterday was really good."

"Was it a good party?" Amai asks.

"Except for one small fight it was an excellent party."

"Who fought who?"

"Maybe I should not call it a fight – it was more of an assault. Musekiwa's wife punched and kicked Razaro quite badly. By the time he left the party, his face was swollen."

"Oh, that woman! Why did she assault her husband's brother like that?" asks Christmas.

"For quite a while, Razaro had been making remarks about women who sleep around with other men when their husbands are away at work in the city. He even sang a mocking song about beating such women. As we all know, Musekiwa's wife has been having an affair with Jekiseni for some time now. Jekiseni was at the party and he knew what Razaro was getting at but pretended not to pay attention. Then Razaro said that if a woman kept on insulting his absent brother's manhood, he was going to kill first the woman and then the man having an affair with her.

"Musekiwa's wife remained silent and kept on sipping her beer slowly. A couple of hours later, she stood up, tied her wraparound cloth more tightly around her, rolled up her sleeves and boldly walked up to Razaro, who was very drunk by then. She apologised to the host for what she was about to do and then began punching Razaro in the face, stomach and all over. He did not fight back and no-one stopped her. It was only when Razaro started vomiting that Musekiwa's wife stopped hitting him. Then she got a bucket of cold water and poured it on him. Afterwards she helped him get up and walked him home to present him to his two wives."

"Aha! And what did the wives say?" Maiguru asks.

"According to Musekiwa's wife, they privately thanked her for a job well done. Then all three women sponged Razaro's swollen face with a tepid cloth and laid him down comfortably on his sleeping mat. Then Musekiwa's wife came back to the party."

"But how is it that Musekiwa's wife gets away with everything?" Christmas asks.

"She grew up on the farm compounds among strong Malawian women who treated their husbands like little boys," says Maiguru.

"Yes, life on the white man's farm demands more than just physical strength from people," says Mai Hilda. "Even if I was on the verge of starvation, I could never work on one of those farms. You may become strong in all kinds of ways, but at the end of many years of hard work you come home with nothing. Look at what happened to my sister-in-law."

I know Mai Hilda's sister-in-law, VaJanet. Three of her sons had gone to school with me until one day they left the village with their mother to join VaJanet's husband on the tobacco farms near Wedza.

"What is life on the white man's farm like?" asks Sis Anna. Could she be thinking of leaving Amai in order to work on the farms?

"Let me tell you," Christmas says, pouring more *chandada* into a mug. He offers it to Sydney knowing full well that Sydney dislikes the twenty-four-hour brew. Sure enough Sydney shakes his head and Christmas continues, "My first farm experience was at Kasora's farm in 1964. *Kasora*, as you know, means 'little weed'. This nickname was given to the white farmer because he would follow workers around on the plantation and whenever he saw that they had missed a little weed, he would shout, *'Kasora!'* and the culprit would have to turn back and pull it out. Men were often kicked in the buttocks if they overlooked weeds but the women were just given warnings.

"A few hours after you got contracted at Kasora's farm, you were expected to build your own makeshift hut of poles thatched with mud. The other workers were always helpful in getting you started, and within a month you were able to follow the routine. Weeding or picking tobacco leaves started at 5:30 a.m. and continued until five in the evening. Women had two hours off to prepare and eat lunch, while men had an hour off for eating.

"The good thing about the farm was that food rations were available. Once a week we were given pieces of meat and bags of maize meal, and farm vegetables were given out twice a week. The pay was very low but we were never without food. Almost every night you could get *chandada*, Malawi gin or *doro*. And there were many divorced or single women available as long as you could pay them. Once you got used to this life of hard work, alcohol and women, you could easily forget about home.

"The school on the farm did not cater for secondary education. And whenever their parents needed help, the children spent their time working rather than in the classroom. When they grew up, many of them stayed on the farm – it was all they knew and they had no education to do anything else.

"VaJanet should never have listened to her husband in the first place. He died on the farm, and their grown-up children will work there and make the white man richer and then come home when they too are old and penniless. I could never have done that."

"Well, you may have left the farm when you were still young, but what is the difference between you and VaJanet?" Mai Hilda asks. "You are just as poor as she is now."

"True. But I have maintained my dignity and I do not have any regrets. No white man ever laid a whip on my back. Why should I have sold my labour for pieces of meat and maize meal?"

"I thought one could make money easily on the farms," Sis Anna says. "If what you say is true, one is better off going to the city to find employment."

"But the city is a terrible place if you are unskilled and unemployed," says Sydney.

"Everything is worth a try. One must never give up without trying." Everyone smiles, sympathising with Sis Anna's hopes of finding a different life for herself.

"Here is the peanut butter. Add it to the vegetables," Mai Hilda says, passing a tablespoonful of peanut butter to Sis Anna.

"Better put on the water for the *sadza*. It is nearly lunch time," Amai says.

"So what is for lunch – other than pumpkin leaves?" asks Sydney.

"Why don't you go and ask your wife?" says Mai Hilda.

"Because I know that Amai makes a better lunch than my wife." For Sydney 'a better lunch' means meat or fish; after a night of drinking, he usually wakes up late and wanders over to Amai's house where she prepares some roast meat to cure his hangover.

Because there are not too many people around today, Amai asks Sydney to open a tin of pilchards to eat with our *sadza*. He knows where the tin is hidden so he quickly finds an opener and disappears into the kitchen.

"A spoilt grown-up son who behaves like a two-year-old!" Mai Hilda exclaims. "When will he realise that he is married and has six children?"

"It does not matter how old they are. An only son living so close to his mother's house will always behave like a little boy. There is no harm in spoiling them while you still have them. These days our sons never seem to reach old age. I have buried three sons and one daughter over the last fifteen years." Maiguru's voice is sad.

"Do not start feeling sorry for yourself again," says Amai. "Sis Anna, is the *sadza* ready?"

"Yes, I am bringing the dish over. But let me warm up the fish first."

In the village, men and women often eat from separate dishes. The *sadza*, accompanied by pumpkin leaves and pilchards, is served on five plates. Christmas shares his with Simba, and as always, Sydney is given his own plate; today he shares with his son, Ruvimbo. Adam shares his *sadza* with Jack, I am to share a plate with Maiguru and Amai, while Sis Anna will eat with Mai Hilda.

But we are rather unfortunate today. Before any of us can eat a morsel, my uncle Zekia's two wives turn up. The food will have to be divided again to accommodate the new arrivals.

"Good afternoon, senior mother," they say to Amai. We all greet them, pretending that we are terribly pleased that they have visited us.

"Do sit down. Do sit down on this mat." My mother makes room for the two women. "You are good farmers. A bad farmer arrives at a place when all the food is gone. But a good farmer will do what you have done – he is excellent at timing exactly when the food is dished out. Here is the dish, my sisters. Do wash your hands and join us."

The two women did not hesitate. "Thank you, senior mother.

We are lucky to get *sadza* with such good relish. In this dry season, vegetables are hard to come by," says one of them.

"I know," says Amai sympathetically.

The women talk as they eat, and I gather that they were not simply passing by – they had set out to visit Amai. Whenever these two turn up together like this, it means that they have an important request to make.

If I were to meet Uncle Zekia in the street, I would not recognise him. He is my father's half-brother – they had the same father but different mothers. It is difficult to keep up with all the uncles and aunts on Baba's side, because my grandfather had five children with my grandmother alone and she was only one of his many wives.

My grandmother's father, Kwenda, was the chief of the land that lay in the valley where my family lived. My grandfather, Grandfather Dickson, was a good Christian man who worked as an interpreter for the Methodist missionaries, and for the first ten years of his marriage, my grandmother and he lived in Chief Kwenda's compound. But then Grandfather Dickson decided to form his own church, which he called the African Zionist Church. As the head of the church, he reasoned, it was up to him to set down the rules. One of the rules he introduced was to allow polygamy. Chief Kwenda, was totally against open polygamy, so he told Sekuru Dickson to have mistresses but not wives. Whereupon my grandfather moved some fifty kilometres to the east where the land was fertile and he could practise his religion without interference.

By the time he died, my grandfather had eight wives and thirty-five children. Some of his wives stayed with him for a few years but eventually went away taking their children with them. As adults, some of the male children returned home to ask for a plot of land on which to build a house in the village. But Uncle Zekia never came back – until a year ago.

For years Uncle Zekia had moved from one job to another. Then he got permanent employment as a butcher in the small town of KweKwe. No longer did he have to worry about relish for his *sadza*: meat was available to him on a daily basis. His white employer even allowed him to take home any leftovers such as bits of fat, ox trotters and tripe. Given this good fortune, it was not long before Uncle Zekia married – three times. The problem came when he could no longer keep three wives and eight children in a small, two-bedroom house. He therefore decided that his two senior wives should go to his village and farm his land. He promised his three wives that they would take turns to live with him in town and that when he got time off, he would visit the wives in the village.

So last year, the two senior wives and their children arrived in the village for the first time with my uncle. He introduced them to his cousins and to the headman. Having proved that he was born in the village and that he was Grandfather Dickson's son, Uncle Zekia was offered a plot of land by the headman. After six weeks, the two wives and their children had built their own two huts, a kitchen hut and a sleeping hut, and could move out from the house of one of the cousins.

The women did everything together: cooked, bathed, took care of the children and even shared the same bed. This was not unusual in the villages, so none of the people raised an eyebrow. The two women slept apart only when Uncle Zekia came home for the weekend. On Friday night his first wife would have the privilege of sleeping with him and then on Saturday it would be the second wife's turn. On Sunday morning, Uncle Zekia would return to the city.

But Zekia did not come home or send his wives money for months on end. The two women would go around the village asking for casual work in return for food, clothing or money. Whenever Amai had work such as weeding or harvesting groundnuts or maize, she asked Uncle Zekia's wives to do it in exchange for clothes. But during the dry season there was hardly any work that needed doing.

"Senior mother, we have to talk to you," one of the wives says. Amai does not reply. Instead, she gets up and asks the two women to follow her to the verandah of the main house where no-one can hear what they have to say. I want to listen to the conversation but decide to stay where I am for a few minutes before going to the big house on some pretext.

"Oh, polygamy! What does it offer women these days except poverty?" says Maiguru. "In the old days, you enjoyed the support of other wives, mothers-in-law and aunts. If your husband favoured one wife over the others, you could complain to the village elders. Not any more."

"But why do these women share a husband in the city, where there are so many men around?" asks Sydney.

"They are fools," Mai Hilda says.

"No. It is because of the increasing poverty in the towns," replies Maiguru. "Women go there looking for employment or a good marriage partner. They fail to get either and end up taking any man who can offer them some form of security."

"They do make some bad mistakes in their selection of men," says Sydney. "I am sure these two have come to complain about Uncle Zekia's neglect of them."

"What can your mother do?" asks Maiguru.

"She is the senior mother of the village so she will listen to their problems and offer them advice. If she cannot help, she will take the matter to the village elders," explains Sydney.

I stroll casually over to the main house, passing the three women on the verandah. Sitting on the couch near the half-open door, I can hear every single word of their conversation. The only problem is that I cannot distinguish between the voices of the two wives. They both speak very fast and give my mother little chance to respond to their complaints.

"He has been home twice in the last six months. On each occasion he left twenty dollars for me and twenty dollars for her, two loaves of bread each and dried beef fat to add to the vegetables. That was all."

"The children are hungry and we also do not have money for school books, uniforms or pencils."

"But that is not the reason why we came here to see you. Tell her, my sister. You tell our senior mother our problem."

"We want the third wife to come and spend time here so that one of us can go to the city for a change. We also want to eat meat with our *sadza*."

"But above all, he has deprived us of the comfort of a man's warmth."

"Yes, when he came here last we took turns to sleep with him, but he did not even stir."

"He no longer wants to treat us as his wives. The first time, I kept it secret from my sister here, thinking that it was my fault. Then, on his second visit, he did the same thing and that is when I told my co-wife here and we both realised that his manhood does not rise. It does not matter what we do to excite him."

"The junior wife has done something to him."

"That is true. She has bewitched him, so that when he comes to us nothing happens."

"Her medicine has weakened him. But when he sees her the

spell disappears and he becomes normal again."

"Senior wife, senior mother, our sister: tell us how we can untie this knot that has weakened our husband."

I am eager to hear Amai's response. I know that for many years now she has no longer believed in spells, love potions or witchcraft, except in very rare cases.

"He may not be bewitched," Amai says. "Maybe he is just tired after the long bus ride home."

"Ah, senior mother! Do not say that. You know very well what a spell can do to a man."

"What do you want me to do? I cannot speak to him because he is not here."

"You do not have to speak to him. Just advise us on what love potion or spell we can use on him, so that when he comes here his manhood will rise for us as well and not just for her."

"My dear young sisters, you have come to the wrong person. I know of no love potion. The only spell I know is to love a man and to perform well in bed."

"That does not work, senior wife."

"I wish I could help. But you must have an idea of what you want to do if your plan fails, because not many women will give you medicine for that sort of thing."

"If we cannot get medicine, then we intend to take turns to go to the town and take the third wife to task. If she does not undo her spell, we will beat her up."

"That is dangerous. My sisters, speak to your husband. Allow him to explain why he is the way he is. Maybe he has another problem which you do not know about."

"Maybe," say the two women. "Thank you, senior wife." They do not sound grateful. They follow my mother back to where the others are; after a few minutes, I go back too.

Jaison has returned from wherever he has been. This time Christmas has not had a chance to hide his beer and so he looks very grumpy. Meanwhile, Jaison talks incessantly about his heroic deeds as a messenger for the freedom fighters during the war. Every now and again Sydney interrupts him, saying, "That is an exaggeration," or "I was there when that happened."

"Two lovely women living by themselves. What a waste of beauty!" Jaison says, looking admiringly at Uncle Zekia's two wives. "If only I was not married, I could sneak in after midnight and keep one of them company."

"You are Zekia's distant nephew. If he were to die today, you would have the traditional right to claim these women as your wives," says Christmas.

"Jaison cannot look after even one wife. How can he be expected to look after two more?" one of the women asks.

"Well, being poor does not mean that one is not a man," replies Jaison. "I can be useful in many ways. Come to think of it, whoever heard of two beautiful women sleeping together? A woman needs a man. That is a fact of life." Jaison takes another big swig at the beer. Christmas watches him, a pained look on his face.

"One of these days," Jaison continues, "I must drop in and see you two women. I will try and hit a lovely fat bird with my catapult and present it to you."

Everyone laughs when he mentions the catapult. "When you see the catapult, ladies, you must flee!" jokes Sydney.

Sis Anna gets busy washing the plates in water drawn from the well. The senior wife washes her hands so that she can relieve Mai Hilda from grinding the peanuts. "Let me do that for you, Aunt," she says. Mai Hilda stands up, yawns hugely and reminds Amai not to forget about the mushrooms she has promised her.

CHAPTER 6

... and Sunday Afternoon

IT IS SUNDAY again and I am back at the homestead. In the valley, several followers of the Apostolic Faith are walking towards the tree where they will hold their service this afternoon. Clad in white robes, they shimmer in the heat, singing a hymn as they go. The *vapostori*, as they are called, follow a very fundamental version of the Old Testament which allows polygamy and other ancient practices. Their churches are springing up under trees everywhere, as life gets harder in this place of drought and poverty. I sit on the verandah, listening to their songs lilting up from the valley.

"People are too religious around here," Sydney scoffs, heading off to seek a quiet spot for his afternoon nap. "Singing all the time to God, as if he has the answers for them."

But I am in the mood to go to church today. Father Francis, the Irish Franciscan missionary, will soon be arriving to set up his makeshift church in the village primary school, offering his own brand of salvation. I decide to go along with Mai Shuvai, Sydney's wife, and see what happens.

Several people have turned up at the school. A few men with old Bibles are gathered under a tree and there are at least forty women sitting around. About half of the women are wearing bright white uniforms and blue caps with white veils and there are rosaries around their necks. This outfit indicates that they are decent married women. The women in ordinary dress are either waiting to be confirmed into the Catholic Church or are unmarried mothers; others do not have any hope of ever wearing the uniform because their husbands will not agree to a Catholic wedding.

I sit among the women in ordinary dress, my dreadlocks covered with a scarf. Father Francis is running late today. Maybe he has been delayed at another village or has had a puncture. We sit and wait for what seems to be hours. I am just about to give up and walk back home when a cloud of dust, rising up way off in the distance, announces the impending arrival of Father Francis's battered old truck. "He is coming!" some teenage girls shout. A man orders us to go into the Grade Six classroom, where benches have been arranged to make pews.

Father Francis has served in this part of the country for more than thirty years. Sydney first met him when Father Francis was teaching at Kutama College. Unlike the rest of us, Sydney went to this Catholic school; later on in life, he would often brag that he attended the same school as President Mugabe.

Before the war, all the schools and churches around our village were either Anglican or Methodist. But when the war started, the freedom fighters condemned all the churches except the Catholic one for collaborating with the colonial exploiters. The Anglican Church came in for particularly severe criticism. "Cecil John Rhodes was a staunch Anglican who preached the gospel of Bible first, then the bullet," the freedom fighters argued in meetings they held in the villages. After one or two such meetings, most village people became Catholics. Even those who sang Anglican hymns secretly in their homes recited the rosary in public.

During the war, Father Francis was working at Gandachibvuva Mission, some fifty kilometres south-east of our village. At night he secretly supplied blankets and food to the freedom fighters. Then one morning the soldiers came to the mission, tortured Father Francis and left him to die. One of the other priests drove him to Salisbury, where he remained in hospital for a month before returning home to Ireland to recuperate.

After independence, Father Francis came back to Gandachibvuva to continue his ministry. He was amazed to find that most Methodists and Anglicans in the area had converted to Catholicism, and that his return was celebrated with much joy by thousands of people. His parish now extended over a fifty-kilometre radius and he came to rely heavily on the assistance of two African priests and five nuns. But despite his busy schedule, Father Francis still managed to visit each village in his parish in turn. In a single Sunday, he could hold four masses at four different villages and then drive his little diesel truck over rough roads back to Gandachibvuva.

Today, Father Francis is accompanied by Sister Immaculate. The women whisper that Sister Anacklet is new and has never been to this school before. Mai Shuvai begins to sing and then all the other voices are raised in unison as Father Francis and Sister Immaculate walk into the classroom; they sit on the two chairs that have been reserved for them behind the table in front. In a corner of the classroom, an old woman plays a drum which is almost as tall as she is. Looking up to the roof as if to heaven, she pounds the drum in ecstasy.

Father Francis has a ruddy, round face which reveals years of exposure to the African sun. His expression is friendly and relaxed, his lips ever ready to curve into a beatific smile. Although he must be close to sixty, he has a good head of hair – no sign of baldness or thinning. I try to imagine what must have caused the young blond boy from Dublin to choose the priesthood and a mission in Africa. Through his dusty brown cassock, I can tell that Father Francis has a bit of a pot belly – years of drinking wine or beer perhaps. On his feet he wears grey socks and comfortable brown sandals.

Sister Immaculate sings and claps her hands. She cannot be more than twenty-five years old – a beautiful, clear-skinned bride of Christ. After the Bible reading, Father Francis asks the young people in the congregation to go into another classroom where Sister Immaculate will talk to them about contemporary issues and spiritual life. The rest of us stay on to listen to Father Francis's sermon, which is delivered in Shona with an Irish accent.

"Jesus will not allow you to continue worshipping other gods. Do you agree with me?" Everyone nods. "I hear many allegations of witchcraft and ancestral worship ceremonies. Even incest among church members has been reported to me. Such abominable acts! And polygamy is also on the increase in the community. How can we hope to prevent the spread of AIDS if we engage in polygamous relationships? My heart bleeds for the little children who are left behind by AIDS victims. If we follow the way of Jesus, we avoid many problems. Let us live upright lives."

For a whole hour, Father Francis speaks relentlessly about many issues: politics, disagreements between husbands and wives, theft, suicide, adultery, illegitimate pregnancies and the evils of abortion and contraception. On several occasions he says, "Finally, I must say this . . ." But then he goes on without stopping.

When at last Father Francis does reach the end of his sermon, his final words are not easy to ignore. "Let us not be misled by the dead. Those who have departed this world are responsible for their own actions. Why should a son or a daughter pay for the sins or crimes of their forefathers? Why should poor Mary or Chiedza be used as human compensation for the murder committed by her father or grandfather? This is evil and unjust in the eyes of God. Dear brothers and sisters, refrain from worshipping ancestral spirits, because among them are those demanding that you pay for their crimes." Father Francis levels his blue-eyed gaze at his flock, pausing for effect. The whole congregation looks down at the floor as if praying. Some people murmur "Amen" awkwardly, as if to fill the heavy silence.

A hot, dry wind lifts the corrugated-iron sheets on the roof of the schoolroom. Dust blows in through the shattered panes of glass in the windows. Father Francis recites the Benediction and then asks the congregation to leave the room and come back one at a time for confession. Everyone queues up outside the classroom, the women in front, and we enter the classroom one by one. The confessions average two to three minutes each. It is not until I am actually kneeling in front of Father Francis, while he recites some words I cannot follow, that I realise that having been brought up a Methodist rather than a Catholic might pose a problem! I quickly decide not to confess about belonging to the wrong denomination.

"Have I seen you before, my child?" Father Francis asks.

I want to say that I am not a child but a mother, and over thirty years of age. But "No, Father," is all I reply.

"Where have you been on Sundays?"

"Around."

"Obviously not in church."

"No."

"Not attending mass is not good in these difficult times." I nod in agreement and Father Francis places his gentle, arthritic hand on my shoulder.

"What sins have you committed against the Lord in word, thought or deed?"

I have a strong desire to say that I have sinned vividly and recently. And I want to confess that during his sermon I had been wondering whether he finds Sister Immaculate attractive. If he was to be tempted, would he resist committing carnal sin with her? Or would he rather entertain more intimate relationships with the African priests? After all these years in Africa, to what extent has he remained faithful to his Catholic principles?

"You are very quiet, my child." I must confess to something if Father Francis is going to let me go. My imagination does not fail me.

"Father, forgive me. I have sinned by often thinking that polygamy is not as bad as we try to make out."

Father Francis chuckles, revealing a good set of false upper teeth, one of his few concessions to white society. "Oh, my child!" He recites more verses and motions me to rise. I actually feel a sense of having been forgiven. I thank Father Francis and make my escape.

When he has heard all the confessions Father Francis moves about among the people, pausing here and there for a chat. He comes over to where I am standing with Mai Shuvai. "Where is your mother-in-law today? I did not see her during confession."

"Oh, she could not attend mass today. She had to see to a sick relative," Mai Shuvai lies. Everyone within earshot knows that my mother is assisting some of the other village women in brewing *doro* at the headman's village. Being so experienced in the final stages of the seven-day brew, Amai has been asked to provide mixing instructions. The beer is being prepared for the *bira* which is to take place tomorrow night – the kind of ceremony that Father Francis has just been sermonising against.

"She would have been here, if not for this untimely illness," Mai Shuvai adds, and some women standing by nod their heads in agreement.

A curious half-smile breaks out on Father Francis's face as he mutters a prayer for the recovery of the 'patient'. He knows very well that the ancestral spirits live alongside the God of Rome here; and he knows my mother well enough to be aware that she would not sit around in church if there is work like brewing to be done.

Father Francis and Sister Immaculate bundle up the pieces of their church: dog-eared hymn books, Xeroxed copies of the sermon and the small bag of coins gathered during the collection. Soon their truck is just a dusty speck on the horizon.

▰▰▰

After the departure of Father Francis and Sister Immaculate, the senior elder of the church tells everyone to sit down so he can make the week's announcements.

"In brief, seeing our time has nearly run out. All members of the youth group are required to attend catechism lessons on Wednesday at 4 p.m. Mai Chipo is not feeling well today, so all church mothers should go to her house and pray for her. The Methodists are planning to revive their church and those who wish to join them can meet here every Sunday at 10 a.m. which means the Catholics can meet at noon. Tomorrow night, the headman wishes to honour the spirit of his grandmother with lots of beer and a beast, so you are all invited to the all-night celebration. Finally, if there are any traditional birth attendants, you are required to go to Java village to attend to a girl who has been in labour for two days. Any more notices?"

There is a long silence. The elder continues, "If those are all the notices, I think we can go home. As for me, I am going to enjoy myself with some very good, warm beer at the headman's house."

On the way home, Mai Shuvai says that everyone in the congregation is likely to attend the *bira* at the headman's house. Father Francis's sermon about ancestral worship does not seem to count for much. Life has been like this for a long time. "The two religions can live comfortably side by side," Baba used to say. "If you try a Western solution and it fails, go back to your traditions. Quite often they do not fail you, because the ancestors understand your problems better than Jesus Christ."

After a few beers, my father would add that it took too long for your messages to get to Jesus. "After all, Jesus is a white man and he has to deal with all the white people's problems first before he gets to the black man." He would explain that there were several interpreters along the line who often made mistakes when translating messages from Shona into English.

"So why bother going to church at all?" we would ask him.

"Because the church offers you an opportunity to see Western civilisation. Through the missionaries, you will learn to speak English. But that alone is not enough to make an African."

Sydney had absorbed a lot of Baba's teachings. But what was he going to pass on to his children? Even in this remote part of the country, where his children had never seen a television set, they worshipped American basketball heroes. Would they grow up to worship the ancestral spirits and participate in traditional rituals, or would the old ways gradually die out in our family?

When we get home, Amai is still not back. But Maiguru is there. She has heard the message from the village across the river asking for help for the young woman who has been in labour for two days. Maiguru, who is a traditional mid-wife, is about to set out. Mai Shuvai and I decide to accompany her.

When we arrive, we find a group of women dressed in white singing outside the young woman's hut: members of the Apostolic Faith, they believe in curing sickness through prayer alone, and are known for shunning doctors and hospitals. Oblivious to our presence, they keep on singing and praying loudly, hoping that their faith will enable the woman to deliver the baby.

"Do not mention that you are a nurse or they will not let you into the house," Mai Shuvai whispers to me. Maiguru and I go into the darkness of the hut. Normally, these mud-brick huts are cool in the heat of the day, but the presence of so many people has made the air stuffy and it is hard to breathe. The young woman in labour is sitting propped against two pillows and a few blankets with her knees up. The baby's head can be seen at the entrance to her vagina. Several women are praying beside the bed, while three elderly women keep urging on the mother-to-be.

"Jessica, push. If you do not push, the baby will never come out," one of them says.

"Please help us," another woman says to Maiguru. "We have been praying for Jessica all night but nothing has happened."

Maiguru washes her hands and kneels beside the patient. I

notice that Jessica is very young – barely sixteen or seventeen. This is her first child. "Obstructed labour requiring forceps delivery," I think to myself.

"Pushing will not help any more," Maiguru says. "Try squatting." The women help the girl to squat, but after half an hour no progress has been made. The praying inside and outside the hut is reaching a crescendo.

"Has she confessed?" Maiguru asks.

"No, no! She is a member of the Apostolic Faith – she cannot confess," says one of the praying women and Jessica shakes her head vigorously.

I am surprised that Maiguru believes in the practice of confession traditionally expected of young girls when they deliver their first babies. According to this belief, a woman can never prove that the father of her first baby is her husband. During labour, if she confesses to having had lovers and names the child's father, the baby is delivered smoothly and easily. For this reason a woman traditionally returns to her parents' village to deliver her first child, so that in case she confesses to infidelities during labour, she does not do so among her husband's relatives.

"Jessica's husband lives in a village not too far from here – some of these women are related to him," another woman says to Maiguru. "If she confesses that she has had an affair, her husband will get to know about it."

Maiguru asks everyone except Jessica's mother to leave the hut. Another hour goes by, and then we hear a baby's screams. All the women ululate with joy.

"A baby boy." Maiguru emerges from the hut, her hands covered in blood. "A very healthy, stubborn boy who wanted to kill himself and his mother by refusing to come out. Where can I get some cow dung?"

"Maiguru, how did you manage to get Jessica to push?" I ask.

"I will tell you later. Just give me some cow dung."

"No, Maiguru, we no longer use cow dung on the umbilical cord," I say. "It can cause tetanus."

"I have used cow dung on umbilical cords for more than thirty years. What is this new disease you are talking about?"

Memories of little babies twitching relentlessly with tetanus cloud my mind. But Maiguru has a determined look on her face and I do not know how to stop her.

"Maiguru, Jessica belongs to the Apostolic Faith. She will not accept any medicine," says Mai Shuvai. The women who are singing agree with her and Maiguru loses the battle.

On the way home, I ask again how she had managed to get the baby out.

"Easy. The girl needed to be told that if she did not confess the names of her lovers, the baby would not come out. Once everyone else was out of the room and only her mother was left, she got all the names out."

"Who did she mention?" I ask. I know that it is against the ethics of the mid-wife to reveal another woman's lovers, but Jessica is not from our village so Maiguru will not mind my question.

"Jessica said that she only slept with her husband once and that was after she had missed a period by two weeks."

"Who is the father, then?"

"Some herd boy called Soromoni. They made love down by the river for several months before and after she got pregnant."

"But why did she marry her husband if she did not love him?" I ask.

"Who marries for love these days? One marries for security, not love. If we only got married for love, then no-one would stay married for long," replies Maiguru. She is walking in front of me, her folded hands resting gently on her bottom. The sun has disappeared behind the Wedza mountains and it is dark. I cannot see where I am stepping, but Maiguru and Mai Shuvai do not seem to have any difficulty avoiding stones and small potholes.

"People fall in love when they first meet," says Mai Shuvai. "They may continue to be in love until after the first child is born. Then they become close friends."

"But Jessica has not been married long. Surely she must care a bit for her husband?"

"Jessica's father is a member of the Apostolic Faith. They strongly believe in polygamy. Remember how in the Old Testament Abraham takes Hagar as a second wife?" Mai Shuvai says.

"Yes."

"Well, it is the same principle. One of the church leaders says that he has been possessed by the spirit and that God has chosen little Jessica, Anna or whoever to go up the mountain with him for a few days. The girl's parents accept the claim and she is sent up the mountain with the elder. When they return, the man says that the Lord has told him to take the girl to be his wife. That is what happened to Jessica."

"Why did she not refuse to go up the mountain?"

"Because she has to obey God's word and her parents as well. But though she could not publicly oppose her parents, she decided to continue her love affair with Soromoni."

"Good for her," I say. My companions do not reply. I wonder whether they too have had affairs. But this is something one never talks about with older women.

When we reach home, Amai is back at last. She tells us of the rich, thick *doro* she has helped make for the ancestors.

"Everybody loves a good beer," she laughs. "Even God.

Perhaps that is why he decided to rest on the seventh day – he knew the home-brew was ready!"

CHAPTER 7

The Death of a Chief

IN THE OLD DAYS, long before the white man came, the king of
this area lived on top of Dengedza mountain, near where our
village is today. Ancient burial sites, grinding stones and pieces
of clay pots have been discovered on the mountain, testimony to
a way of life that has long since disappeared. The royal dwelling
stood amongst the granite rocks at the very summit. The thirty
to forty members of the king's household took care of all his
needs, which meant that the monarch never needed to leave the
mountain. From his hilltop throne, he could look out over the
lands where his cattle, his community's wealth, were grazed. On
top of the hill were stone walls, behind which the king could
walk observed only by the sentries posted there to warn of any
impending attacks. Ceremonies were held in a natural
amphitheatre, whose rocky walls were painted with images
depicting hunts, ceremonies and scenes from daily life.

The coming of the white man spelt the end for the regional
monarchs and chieftains. Stripped of their authority, they
became the puppets of the white district administrators, willing
to keep their subjects in line in return for special favours, such
as supplies of the white man's alcohol and tobacco. And inde-

pendence from the colonial regime brought increasing centralisation of government and reduced the role of the traditional rulers even further. Although a village chief or headman still had the right to distribute land to newcomers and settle disputes, the sweeping powers of the kings of the past were gone forever.

▲▲▲

I recognised Chifamba the moment he walked through our homestead gate. Most people would tell you that you only needed to meet Chifamba once for his image to stay with you for the rest of your life. He was nicknamed Demo, which means axehead. It was surprising that he had survived his birth: his mother had been in labour for two days before an old mid-wife pulled the infant out by the head. The other women tried to mould the baby's head into a normal shape – but to no avail. Chifamba was destined to have an axe-like head. When he was being thrust onto the breast, his mother noticed that poor little Demo had clubbed feet as well. Again, the mid-wives tried to help but they couldn't straighten the baby's feet. As a teenager, Chifamba would spend hours making his own sandals from old car tyres. At school no-one dared tease him about his disability because he was renowned as a good fighter.

Chifamba's father was old Chief Kwenda, my grandmother VaKariwo's brother. Many women threw themselves at Chifamba, but he showed little interest in them. If he lived in the West, people would have called him a homosexual; in Africa, he was known as a senior bachelor. It was rumoured that Chifamba was possessed by a *svikiro*, an ancestor who disliked women. He spent most of his time herding cattle with young men even when he was considered too old to go down to the valley with the boys.

Despite his antipathy to marriage, Chifamba was well liked in the village. In my family we knew him as the messenger who brought news of death or special ceremonies to my mother, so his arrival was always taken very seriously. He visited us once or twice a year and rarely brought good news.

In no hurry to share his latest secret with us, Chifamba asked for food and tea after running through the normal greetings. A few minutes later, he was sitting drinking hot sweet tea by the fire and eating sweet potatoes. Amai and Sydney talked to him about the recent harvest and other unimportant things, trying to find out what his news could be.

Chifamba suddenly said, "I have some news of great concern."

"I am the oldest grandson of VaKariwo and Amai here is the senior daughter-in-law to your family. You are here because your problems are our problems," Sydney said, using his best patriarchal voice.

"Do not tell me what I already know," Chifamba replied. "The news I bring with me today is not good. I have been asked to come and tell you that the old chief, my father, is very ill indeed."

Amai and Sydney remained silent. They had been expecting to hear this at any time during the past ten years. Some twenty years before, my grandmother had been summoned to the chief's bedside after he had fallen from the roof of a hut he was thatching. Everyone thought he would die, but he had only broken a leg and went on to outlive both my grandparents and my father too.

"He has been seriously ill for a week," Chifamba continued. "The chances of survival are very slim. You, my aunt's daughter-in-law and the wife of my father's nephew, are therefore required to attend to him in his illness. It is your duty to see that he peacefully goes to join the ancestors without too much trouble."

Chifamba reached into his jacket and pulled out a snuff container made from the horn of an ox. He poured a small amount of snuff into the palm of his left hand, took a pinch between his right thumb and finger and pushed it into his nostrils. Then, using both nostrils, he inhaled all the snuff off his palm. He sneezed twice, took a deep breath and relaxed his shoulders.

"Uncle, we have heard your message," said Sydney. "For many years you have carried messages back and forth between our grandmother's home and ours. But as you know, I have several commitments at the school so I cannot come and attend to your father's illness."

"I did not come to get you. What would I need a man for at this stage? If the chief wishes to relieve himself and cannot walk to the bush, will you give him a bedpan?" Chifamba asked with some irritation.

"Cousin," my mother intervened, "the young man speaks with too much haste. He does not understand my role."

"That is true. The ignorance of your Western-educated children will ruin us. Explain the custom of the people to your stupid son."

"According to tradition," began Amai, "the illness of a chief is kept secret except among his immediate family. All his nursing care is provided by the women who have married his nephews, since these women are not directly related to him through blood ties. In the chief's case, I am the wife of his senior nephew. Therefore I am responsible for all his needs and I am allowed to see his nakedness. Like a faithful nurse, I will sit by his bedside day in day out for as long as I am wanted. The chief will tell me his deepest secrets and also instruct me on a number of matters that he wants me to pass on to members of his family. Do you understand now?"

"Oh, yes," said Sydney. "Forgive me, Uncle. When do you wish to leave with Amai?"

"As soon as possible," replied Chifamba. "I know buses from this place leave when the first rooster crows. I am required to take your mother to the chief by tomorrow afternoon."

The next day, Amai and Chifamba caught the 4 a.m. bus and arrived at Chief Kwenda's house not long after sunrise. The chief's two wives welcomed my mother quietly and led her into the large *rondavel* where the old man lay on his single bed. Amai knelt on the cow-dung-polished floor, called the chief by his totem and then announced who she was. The chief lifted a skinny arm and shook Amai's hand.

"My nephew David's dear wife! The one who David left when she was still young enough to bear him more children. How I wished I had died in his place," he said weakly.

"*Aika!* Why do you speak of the departed at this hour? Let us focus on the present. How are you, Uncle?"

"This is what you see."

"He has hardly eaten," said one of his wives. "Maybe you could get him to eat something."

Three other women were assigned to help my mother nurse the chief. As senior nurse, she could tell them what to do. Towards evening she asked one of her assistants to bring her a dish of herbal leaves which had been soaked in boiling water. With his head under a blanket, the chief breathed in the strong-smelling steam. He sweated and coughed, but my mother encouraged him to persist and a few minutes later he lay back on his pillows, stopped coughing and fell asleep.

All night my mother kept watch over the chief and attended

106

to his needs. Shortly after midnight, he seemed to be gaining strength and started talking as if there was nothing wrong with him. Amai knew that when death approaches it can fool the dying, making them speak with sudden energy and enthusiasm. She sat and listened to the chief talk of events long past as if they had happened the day before.

"The most beautiful time in my life was when I was a young man, herding cattle. All the young men my age took the cattle down to the valley. We did not come back till after sunset. We feared nothing except hyenas, lions and snakes. Hunger was unheard of in those days. How could we go hungry when there were so many wild fruits to eat? And plenty of cow's milk and goat's milk to drink.

"Occasionally, some girls would come by and we would chase them around the valley. If the girls were not strong enough to resist our male power, they got pregnant. But no young man ever turned a woman's pregnancy away. If a girl said you were responsible for her pregnancy, then you were a proud man indeed. The country was so beautiful and so peaceful . . . there were many trees then . . . now the trees are gone and the land is sliding away from under our very feet . . ."

The chief had dozed off. Amai pulled the blankets over his shoulders and turned him on his side. She spread a goatskin mat on the floor at the foot of the bed and made herself comfortable. The other three women were already lying around the bed sound asleep.

But Amai could not sleep. A sixth sense told her that the chief was unlikely to wake up. At dawn she felt the old man's hand. It was cold. She tried to gently move his head and felt how stiff it was. The chief of the Vanjanja people was dead.

As was the custom, my mother and the three other nurses

bathed the body and oiled it. They dressed the chief in his best clothes and quietly went to tell the elders of the village that the chief's spirit had seen fit to join those who went before him. The elders gathered secretly to discuss the burial procedures in hushed tones.

That day, life in the chief's village went on as normal. Children played, women fetched water and cooked meals as if nothing had happened. Tradition demands that a chief's death be kept secret for at least two months. His body is carried away by relatives at night and laid to rest in a cave next to his predecessors. Only senior members of his family are allowed to know the chief's final resting place. And only when a successor has been chosen is it announced that the chief is dead. People do not ask when he died or where he is buried. Instead they come in hundreds to mourn him as if he had just died.

For Chief Kwenda to be buried next to his forefathers was not going to be easy. The first Chief Kwenda had died in the early 1930s, when his family lived near present-day Harare, and was buried in the traditional royal burying place somewhere in the mountains. Then in 1933, the colonial government introduced the Land Apportionment Act, which segregated Africans to what was called the Tribal Trust Lands, thus excluding them from most of the fertile land which was reserved for white farmers. The chief's family had to move to the valley where his descendants now lived. Although the new place of settlement was not very fertile, it was virgin land with lots of hills and trees. In 1970 when the next Chief Kwenda, my great-grandfather, died, it was not difficult to find a hiding place among the hills. But twenty-six years later, all the trees were gone, cut down for firewood, and there were only shrubs left. People had to travel as far as twenty or thirty kilometres in search of firewood, further and further each year. The government had begun a reforestation programme in an effort to prevent the area from becoming a desert in a couple of decades. But that was no help to the elders who had to decide where to bury the chief.

"Where shall we bury my father?" Chifamba was heard whispering this question to many elders of the clan. "There are no hiding places left."

While she waited for the elders to make a decision on where to bury the chief, Amai applied peanut butter oil to the body every few hours. People passing by the chief's home were greeted with the usual friendliness.

"How is the big father this morning?" asked one passer-by.

"Doing fine. In fact, he has gone down to the river to immerse his poor old bones in cold water," came the reply.

In the evening, the elders gathered again. This time all the senior women were invited to participate and offer advice.

"This morning I went to check the old burying place up in what used to be the big hills," Chifamba began. "There is not a single tree left. All you can see are some thorny shrubs leading to the cave where the old chief lies. Fortunately, people do not trespass into the cave for fear of cobras and black mamba."

"That is not the only reason why people have not entered that dark cave," the chief's senior wife said.

"What do you mean?" asked Chifamba.

"Don't you remember that during the war the bodies of a couple of white soldiers were thrown in there and buried overnight by the comrades? Up to this very day, our chief lies next to two strangers whose totems we do not know. It is an abomination.

"Sometimes, late on dark nights, the two white men's ghosts are seen walking the hills," the senior wife continued. "You can hear them speaking English to each other. Obviously, their spirits are troubled. They want to be buried among their own people."

"We did not gather to talk about foreign spirits. Let us focus on why we are here," said one of the men. For a long time, the discussions and arguments went on. Some said that it was no longer possible to conceal the death of the chief. Others said that Chief Kwenda should be buried openly because once or twice during his life he had called himself a Christian; since Christians do not believe in ancestral spirits, the chief should be buried in the Christian way, they argued. Still others held that whether the chief was a Christian or not did not matter – what was important was his role as a traditional leader. Burying him as a Christian would be an insult to the ancestors.

"If he joins Jesus and the angels, who will listen to us when we offer beer and meat to his spirit?" argued one of the elders. "We must bury the chief in the same way we have done with the others for many generations."

"Yes, we should follow tradition. But how can we do it when our land is so barren and there are no hidden caves left?" Chifamba asked.

"The only secret place I know is the underground space beneath the senior wife's kitchen," the chief's second wife said.

"What underground place are you talking about?" asked the senior wife.

"It is simple," replied the second wife. "We dig deep, deep down through the floor of your hut and make a grave. Then he is buried in this and the hut is permanently locked."

After further discussion, it was agreed that the second wife had come up with the best solution. By dawn, the pit had been dug. The women sang traditional burial songs softly as the old chief was lowered into the grave. Then Chifamba knelt down and apologised at length to the dead spirit, explaining why his people had departed from the old custom.

"My dear father," Chifamba said, while everyone listened, "we wanted to bury you among your people. Many years ago it would have been possible for us to unite you with older members of the clan whose bones now lie in the white man's country. But if we attempt to go to those caves, we will be arrested for trespassing on private property. Things have changed. Your own father sleeps with the foreigners. Please accept that we have done all we can to try to follow the traditional path, but it is no longer possible. The hills are naked without the trees. The wild animals have fled and the country has been left bare. How are we to save it? How can we find a proper burial place for you? Forgive us for burying you like a commoner. But this is the best place we could find. At least we will continue to pay homage to you knowing that your spirit is right here in the village. Go well, my father."

The men clapped hands and the women ululated. Then the group quietly dispersed, leaving Amai and her three assistants to polish the floor of the hut with cow dung mixed with ground charcoal. By sunrise the senior wife's kitchen had been locked and her cooking utensils shifted into the second wife's hut.

"I must return home," Amai announced to the elders that afternoon.

"We thank you for your service," said Chifamba.

"But thanking me by word of mouth is meaningless," said Amai. She knelt down, and her three assistants knelt in the dust next to her.

"We will not move until you recognise our duties," said one of the assistants.

"But we are poor," said Chifamba.

"We will not move," replied my mother. The four women made themselves comfortable and talked casually to each other. Every now and again they laughed and clapped each other's hands.

It was the custom that these women be given a present to show appreciation for their labour. A while later, two boys arrived with a goat and three chickens. Chifamba went down on one knee and said to Amai, "Here is your goat. Share it with your sisters and take some of the meat home and eat it with the children. You performed a great task. To witness the nakedness of a chief is not done easily. Also, to wash his dead body can only be done by one who has come from a different clan, such as yourself."

My mother and her three assistants danced and ululated. "Our relish, my sisters," said Amai. She gave each assistant a chicken, then placed her hand on the goat's back and said, "What a healthy fat goat this is. Thank you, Chifamba. Despite your clubbed feet, narrow brain and hatred for women, you do think like a man."

The women laughed and so did Chifamba.

"Here, my sisters, let us find someone to kill the goat. Then I will divide it into portions so we can share it among ourselves," said my mother.

Chifamba sharpened his blunt knife and led the goat away. After killing and skinning it, he asked Amai to instruct him on how to share out the pieces. She took both thighs, offered Chifamba the head, the feet and the skin, and divided the rest between her assistants.

Before sunset my mother was waiting at the bus stop, accompanied by the senior wife and Chifamba.

"In a couple of months I shall visit you again, with news about when we want to announce the chief's death," Chifamba said.

"I shall be waiting for the celebration. Next time, you will not give me a goat for my services – I will demand a cow," Amai laughed as the bus approached.

▲▲▲

Back home, my mother kept the death of the chief secret from everyone except the members of her immediate family. I wondered what would happen when the next chief died. Already all the burial places were gone and in any case the customs were being forgotten. Maybe one day people would forget where Chief Kwenda was buried and knock down the hut that served as his tombstone. They might even build a chicken run or a cattle kraal on top of the old chief.

"What would happen if a chief were to die in hospital?" I asked Amai one day, a few weeks later.

"A chief should not die in hospital," she replied.

"But it has happened," Sydney joined in. "Somewhere near Masvingo, a chief was dying from cancer of the throat. He was hospitalised for weeks and one night he died. According to the story, a nurse on night shift rang the police station and asked them to communicate the death to his family. The police officer managed to get through to the district council offices near the chief's house the following day. He spoke to a junior clerk, who quickly shouted to a group of women sitting under a tree nearby, 'Is there anyone from Chief So-and-So's village? If there is, can she please come here.' A young woman who happened to be the chief's grand-daughter followed the clerk into the office, where he told her to run to the chief's residence and tell the people that their chief was no more. On receiving the news, the young woman ran screaming out of the council offices and shouted that the chief was dead. All the women broke into hysterics."

"Silly woman!" Christmas said.

"No, she was not silly," replied Sydney. "If you look at this story closely, you will see that the first people to make a mistake were those who took the chief to the hospital. Western medicine should not be allowed to intervene in the illness of a chief."

"But some chiefs die from AIDS," pointed out Amai. "Others die in car accidents, others from too much alcohol. These are Western diseases, so why should a chief not go to hospital?"

"True. But in the village, people are saying that the old kings are looking down from Dengedza, brooding over what has happened in their lands. The old ways are being forgotten, the rains have stopped coming, the soil is blowing away – and even death no longer follows the traditions."

CHAPTER 8

Disputes

ROZINA, AMOSI'S wife, had not spoken for three days. She sat in her hut with her back to the wall, legs stretched out in front of her and eyes fixed into space. Her face was expressionless. For three days Amosi, his mother and other close relatives tried hard to discover what was wrong with Rozina. But she would not eat, speak or move. Her two-year-old son played outside and whenever he felt hungry, he would come into the hut, lift up his mother's blouse, suck at her breast for a little while and then go back out to play. His pleas for more milk were ignored by Rozina.

"Daughter-in-law, you will die of hunger," Amosi's mother said. "Will you please tell us what eats your heart? Where is the pain?"

Rozina said nothing.

"I do not think she is in pain," said Amosi. "She may be possessed by an evil spirit."

Amosi's mother was in her late seventies. Her husband had died a long time ago, before Amosi, her youngest son, got married. For a short while during the war, Amosi left the village and joined the Rhodesian Army, but after independence he came home to stay. It was rumoured that he occasionally caught the bus to Mbare market in Harare where he would spend a week stealing travellers' purses. Everyone in the village knew about these little visits to the city. For years his wife had asked Amosi to look for acceptable employment but he preferred to steal, drink and smoke. He hardly ever helped her in the fields, nor did he contribute anything to the family's upkeep. Yet he remained his mother's favourite son.

On the afternoon of the third day of Rozina's silence, Amosi's mother came to visit Amai. "Mai Sydney, David's wife, Shuvai's grandmother, I have come," the old lady saluted my mother.

"You are welcome," said Amai.

"You have heard about my daughter-in-law's illness?"

"Yes. For how long has Rozina been silent now?"

"When the sun sets this evening, it will be the third night."

"How did it all start?"

"I am not sure. According to Amosi, Rozina went to visit her mother last Sunday. When she came back, she was quite normal. Then on Wednesday morning she got up very early, went down to the river and bathed herself. She fetched three buckets of water and placed two bundles of firewood near her hut. After giving the children some porridge to eat, she had a small argument with Amosi over his lazy habits. Apparently one of the goats had been missing for a week and Amosi had done nothing about it. Then she simply sat down in her hut and refused to move, speak or do anything. Tell me what to do, wife of my uncle."

Puzzled, Amai shook her head. Then, after a long pause, she smiled. "Ah, Mai Amosi, can't you see what Rozina is doing? She is staging a silent *bopoto*."

"But that cannot be correct," said Mai Amosi. "Rozina is a young woman. What does she know about *bopoto* that she should stage one in my son's house? She really cannot do that to me. Anyway, according to my understanding, it is only a *bopoto* if the woman makes a lot of noise."

"Remember my *bopoto*?"

"Who can forget that?" The two elderly women laughed together.

▰▰▰

Even I could remember Amai's *bopoto*. That was the year our family moved away from the main village and Amai began moulding bricks to build the present homestead. One morning, well before sunrise, I heard her shouting some very angry words at the top of her voice. Peering out through the window, I saw Amai standing in the front yard. She had her skirts lifted up, revealing her brown legs.

I woke up Phaina, my oldest sister, and asked her what the noise was all about. "Amai is staging a *bopoto*," she replied, peering through the window.

"What is that?" I asked.

"A *bopoto* is when you make angry noises and tell everyone that you have been badly mistreated," Phaina explained. "Amai is angry with Sekuru Dickson."

We all knew that when Grandfather Dickson married his seventh wife, there weren't enough plots of land for everyone to farm. So he simply took an acre of land from Amai and gave it to his new wife. This left Amai without a piece of land to grow groundnuts. She sought assistance from our grandmother and other village elders but no-one showed much interest in the case. Grandfather Dickson argued that as Baba was a teacher, he generated enough income to buy peanut butter for his family. His reasoning was regarded by most villagers as unfair and ridiculous, but no-one dared oppose Grandfather Dickson. After all he was the village headman and could allocate land as he wished.

The only channel through which Amai's complaint could be heard was a *bopoto* – a form of speaking out in protest which was the traditional resort of women with grievances.

We children dressed, went outside and watched Amai marching around her hut with her skirts raised. We had never seen her so angry or heard her speak so loudly.

"When I first came to this village, I was introduced to you as the father of my husband. From the very moment I set my eyes on you, you became my father. I was introduced to my husband's mother and she became my mother. All my husband's people became my people. I expected you to treat me the same way you would treat your own daughter. But then when I delivered my first-born child, you did not visit my house until the child had started to walk. It was a girl child, you said bitterly, and you wanted your first grandchild to be a boy. When you refused to see my newborn baby I did not complain. Instead, I kept quiet.

"Then the rains came. You knew that my husband and I had no oxen to plough the fields. It was your responsibility to provide us with some animals. But you did not offer me any help until everyone's fields except mine had been ploughed. By the time I sowed the first seeds, the ground was dry and some people had already commenced weeding. That year, I harvested crops from land I had dug with my bare arms. But did I complain against my father-in-law? No. I remained silent.

"Then your third wife's daughter died at the age of six months. You secretly called me a witch and blamed me for the baby's death. You did not come to speak to me directly. All this was hearsay which I did not believe for a while. But when I realised that you had stopped eating or drinking in my house, I knew it was true you thought I was a witch. Still I remained quiet because one does not ask one's father-in-law about gossip.

"Five years ago, my son Sydney ate some poisonous mushrooms. I did not think that he was going to survive. You came to pray for him with members of your Zionist church. When your prayers failed to cure him, you asked if one of your healers could take him home and care for him. I said that I preferred to take him to hospital. Who does not know that people can die from mushroom-poisoning? Maybe prayers help, but I was not going to let you take my son away. I asked to use your bicycle to take my son to the clinic because it was so far away. You turned down my request and called me a disobedient heathen. Your wife and I took turns in carrying Sydney on our backs until we reached the clinic. The boy was nearly dead from vomiting. He was in hospital for two weeks. My son came so close to dying. But I did not complain that you refused to lend me your bicycle. It was a man's bicycle, you said, and women might menstruate on it. But I did not complain, did I? One does not easily challenge one's father-in-law.

"For many years I tried to avoid any misunderstanding between us. Now the rains have come again. I have enough oxen to plough the fields. My children are all healthy and strong. They can help me work on the land. Last year I harvested seven bags of groundnuts from my groundnut field. All year I have made peanut butter and added it to the children's porridge. I even made peanut oil for cooking and also for oiling the children's bodies. During the dry season I dug manure from the cattle pen, from the chicken house and from my rubbish pit so I could spread it over my groundnut field. Now the field is ready for ploughing and I have my seeds ready. But what do you do to me? You take away my field and give it to your wife. Does she know how much time I have spent caring for that field during the last sixteen years? Do you know that a groundnut field is a woman's pride? My father-in-law, you have insulted my womanhood for too long. Taking away my groundnut field is the last straw. I want everyone to know that I can no longer accept being trodden upon like dirt."

Amai's voice could be heard for quite some distance; even people from across the river had heard her shouting and had gathered in our yard. By breakfast time, a large group of people were sitting there listening to Amai, who did not stop shouting out her grievances.

Then Grandmother Kariwo appeared, listened briefly and disappeared again. She returned a few minutes later followed by Grandfather Dickson, who seemed to be half-asleep; he had been dragged away from the arms of his latest young bride. Grandmother Kariwo was speaking quickly, gesturing with her hands and pointing to Amai and the people gathered round. Some elders took my grandfather aside and talked to him in hushed tones. Then they called Grandmother Kariwo to them and we saw her nod her head several times. She left the elders and approached Amai.

"Our daughter, we have heard your grievances," Grandmother Kariwo said, kneeling in front of my mother. "We beg you to calm down."

Amai lowered her skirts but kept on marching around her hut.

"Your father and all the elders are here. Please let the people disperse and we will talk about it among ourselves."

Amai followed Grandmother Kariwo to where the men were sitting. A long discussion followed. By late afternoon, the crisis had been resolved. Amai could be seen happily spreading some manure from our rubbish pit on her groundnut field.

━▲▲▲━

"You never staged another *bopoto* after that," Amosi's mother said.

"There was no need to do so. And you can only stage one *bopoto*. If you do several, the people will ignore you."

"That is true. So you think Rozina is staging one?"

"Yes."

"But she is silent."

"A *bopoto* is not always vocal. Some women may choose silence. What Rozina wants now is to attract a crowd. Then she will speak," said my mother.

Amai and I accompanied Mai Amosi back to Rozina's hut. Several villagers had gathered outside. Amosi kept on telling them that his wife had had a stroke. "If I had transport, I would take her to hospital," he said.

"She is not sick. Look at her – her face shows some very deep grievances," said Amosi's mother. She explained that Rozina's emotional anguish had caused her to stage a silent *bopoto*. Then she asked whether VaMonica, Amosi's grandmother, was present.

"She has been called," someone replied.

A few minutes later, VaMonica arrived and Amosi's mother came forward to greet her.

"It is good to see you here. I should have sent a child to get you but I thought Rozina was genuinely sick. So I went to see Mai Sydney for some medicine."

VaMonica went into Rozina's hut and knelt down. She spoke to Rozina for a long time while everyone waited outside. Then, through the open door of the hut, we saw Rozina slowly get up and stretch. She came outside and saw us all sitting there. Then she started speaking.

She began by talking about how Amosi courted her, their marriage ceremony and the birth of their four children. Then she went on: "We all know that it is difficult to find a job in town. But other men still go and spend six months looking for work and come home only when they have utterly failed to find any. Amosi has not looked for a job since the war. I work in the fields and get paid for weeding other people's land. If I earn five dollars, Amosi takes it away and buys beer. If I complain, he beats me up. See this scar?" She pointed to a cut on her cheek. "When I married Amosi, I did not have this scar."

People mumbled and shook their heads.

"You could all say that women do get beaten up often. But I want to say that I do not want to be assaulted any more. Several times I have spoken to Amosi's mother about this treatment. But all she has said is that it is normal for a man to beat his wife. Yet she boasts that in all her married life, her husband never assaulted her. So why should I be subjected to such treatment?"

Rozina paused. Some men said that surely being beaten for complaining was not serious enough to warrant a *bopoto*. Rozina disagreed.

"I am not standing here to complain about one simple matter. Last week, I discovered that Amosi was preparing to pay two cows in order to marry a young woman he has already made pregnant."

"Who is this woman?" someone asked.

"Ask Amosi or his mother. They know."

Amosi and his mother kept their heads down.

"Tell me, if another woman comes to live here with us, how

are we going to survive?"

A couple of men laughed and one of them said, "Oh, these days, women make a lot of noise out of nothing. This is child's play. Whoever heard of a woman making such a big deal out of wife-beating and polygamy? This is part of our culture. It is something that we have lived with for many years. Woman, you have abused a woman's right to speak."

The man who said this rose up and left. Two others followed him.

"But why should Rozina suffer so much?" asked her aunt, who lived nearby. "Why should she not complain if she has been subjected to physical and emotional abuse? Daughter of my brother, if these people do not want to listen to you, pack your bags and return to your parents. In these days of *hedzi*, who wants to sleep with a man who takes just anyone as a bedmate? Why should Amosi kill you? As if the suffering he has already inflicted on you is not enough.

"It is not easy for a woman to stage a *bopoto*. When Rozina stopped eating or talking, it was not her wish. Sometimes the anger inside takes control of your ability to do anything. This anger would have suffocated Rozina if she did not speak out."

VaMonica then stood up. In an authoritative voice, she said: "Rozina, we have heard your problem. At some stage in our married lives, we have all felt the same. These days, not many women stage a *bopoto*. If you were in the city, they would probably have locked you up in a psychiatric hospital thinking that you were mad. But we know that you have a genuine problem.

"In the old days I would have said that polygamy gives the senior wife a lot of respect. I would have also celebrated the birth of more children. But these days, who can afford to feed several children in one house? The rain no longer pours the way it used to do. Our land is so poor and unproductive. What is the point of adding more mouths to feed, when you yourself can barely survive on what you have? My grandson here is a foolish man and everyone knows that. But let us not waste our time listening to this problem – this is an issue between three people. Rozina: you, your mother-in-law and your husband must address your grievances. This is an issue between you three people."

VaMonica sat down and started taking some snuff. The crowd dispersed and left Rozina with her mother-in-law and Amosi to discuss the problem.

▰▲▰

A couple of months later, I learnt that Amosi had gone ahead and married a second wife. Rozina had taken their youngest child and returned to her parents.

"Now Amosi's mother has to care for her three older grand-children. What a foolish woman!" said Amai. "A sensible mother should never support polygamy these days. Those children are going to starve. Only yesterday I saw Amosi and his mother coming back from a beer party well after sunset. The second wife cannot be expected to be a good mother to Rozina's children."

"But why did she marry Amosi if she did not want to be a stepmother?" I asked.

"She married Amosi so that she could enjoy the competition between herself and Rozina," replied Amai. "Some women enjoy conflict. You wait and see, she is not going to last very long – for her, a marriage without competition with another woman is not exciting enough. Meanwhile, we must keep our doors locked at night because Amosi is bound to go around the village looking for something to steal."

Although there were rules governing property, petty theft was not unusual in the village. A few people were well known for stealing little things such as chickens, eggs or sweetcorn from yards and fields. Time and time again, these offenders would appear in front of the chief. Amosi was one of the men who were continuously being disciplined by the chief's court.

I did not realise that I was going to be Amosi's next target. But one day, my beautiful handpainted bedspread and two tins of spaghetti were missing from my mother's house. Simba saw an empty spaghetti tin in Amosi's rubbish pit and became suspicious. He went into Amosi's house and found the second wife busy: she had cut up my bedspread into small pieces which she was sewing into clothes for her stepchildren.

Simba reported all this to my mother and the matter was taken to the local chief's court. Amai told me that I should attend the court hearing, as she could not attend it herself since what had been stolen did not belong to her. The truth was that Amai had been to Chief Matambo's court several times over the years, accusing Amosi of having stolen from her; she had never recovered any of her property and did not want to waste any more time at court hearings.

Two days before the hearing, the chief's policeman, Takesure, went to Amosi's house to deliver a handwritten note to him. Amosi was at home smoking *mbanje* (marijuana). Although this was illegal, he did not make any attempt to hide what he was doing. In fact he offered Takesure a couple of joints and the two of them sat smoking quietly for some time. Takesure complimented Amosi on having grown such a good crop and Amosi explained that it was his new wife who had faithfully cared for the plants. Takesure and Amosi then shared a mug of beer and joked for a while about different things, after which Takesure left.

He stopped at our homestead, told Simba about his morning with Amosi and reminded me that I could be charged with contempt of court if I did not appear before the chief on Wednesday.

"What time should I be there?" I asked.

"Ten o'clock," said Takesure.

"That means midday – or sometime after lunch," laughed Sydney.

Simba was to accompany me as my main witness. On Wednesday morning, we walked the five kilometres down to the Save valley where Chief Matambo lived. His impressive compound contained two granaries and several thatched huts, shaded by mango, mulberry and peach trees. This was obviously a long-established homestead – at least fifty years old.

A young woman directed us to the chief's court, which was held behind the huts. Between thirty and forty people were sitting under the shade of a big *msasa* tree: the women sat apart from the men on goatskin mats or on their wraparound cloths, legs outstretched; most of the men were seated on two huge logs; and in the middle of the two groups sat Chief Matambo and his advisers. The chief presided over his court sitting in a hand-carved chief's chair and wearing a leopard skin over his white shirt and tie; his three advisers were seated on homemade stools.

Simba and I discovered that our case was number four on the court's list that day – it would not be heard until that afternoon. Takesure was just calling for the witnesses in the first case.

With his khaki uniform and military bearing, Takesure could have been mistaken for an army officer. He was about six feet tall and had a moustache which he twisted at the ends so that he could look more like an English colonel. On his head he wore a pith helmet – the type used by the King's African Rifles during colonial days. In his right trouser pocket, he kept a pair of silver handcuffs which he used occasionally when an offender became unco-operative; he also carried a short, thick stick for hitting people on the head if necessary. Although he could not resist the temptation of marijuana, he was a well-respected man of the law who did not entertain any misconduct in Chief Matambo's domain.

The first case involved a man in his fifties called Chigondo, who had been caught committing adultery with Matare's wife, Chimhosva. Chimhosva, who must have been in her late forties, was sitting between the two men.

"Matare, you have come before us with a crime that has been committed against you," said Chief Matambo.

"Yes, Chief. I stand before you today because another man has dared to insult my manhood," said Matare, rising to his feet.

"What crime was committed against you?"

"The man standing with me in front of you is the offender, Your Honour. His name is Chigondo, and he is of the Vahera clan. As you well know, Chigondo's mother also belongs to the Vahera clan and so does my wife. By dishonouring my wife, Chigondo has also dishonoured his own mother."

"That is beside the point," said the chief. "Just tell me in detail how Chigondo has abused your manhood. But first, Takesure, tell the audience that if there are any people present who are related to each other and are likely to be embarrassed by the interrogation that will take place, they should leave us now. These kinds of cases can involve some embarrassing references to sexual matters."

Takesure saluted the chief. "If there is a mother-in-law and her son-in-law here, or if there are any brothers and sisters, or if there is anyone who gets embarrassed about issues concerning the way we live as people, I ask them to leave us for a while."

Five people, two women and three men, left the court. Then Matare launched into the details of his case.

"Your Honour, there were some people drinking at Mai Amosi's place. Chigondo arrived with three large mugs of beer which we drank together. Before the beer was finished, Chigondo said that he had to go home and check if his children had managed to locate his missing bull. You all know about Chigondo's bull – the one that destroys people's crops all the time?"

"Yes, we do," said Takesure impatiently.

"I was so grateful for the beer that I decided to stay and drink until it was all finished. But a few minutes after Chigondo left, someone, I will not mention names, someone joked about a bull that was human. I took no notice. That person then went on to call me a bull without horns. Now that made me angry and I would have punched the person for mocking me if another person, this time a woman, had not said to me, 'Leave him alone, Matare. If you were a bull, you would not let another bull sleep with your wife in exchange for a few mugs of beer.'

"That made me really angry but I did not want to fight with anyone. As you know, Your Honour, I am a peaceful man. So I controlled my anger and kept drinking, but I left before the beer ran out."

"Yes, he left the rest of the mug to me," called out Amosi.

"No-one asked you!" Takesure prodded Amosi in the back with his stick.

"When I walked into my courtyard, I decided to urinate next to my bedroom window," continued Matare. "Then something stopped me. For a few seconds I thought I was dreaming. Surely that was not a man's voice in my bedroom! I listened carefully – sure enough, there was a man in my bedroom. Because the window was half-open, I could hear all the noises."

"What noises?" asked a man in the audience. Matare looked at his feet and mumbled something softly.

"Matare, you are not talking to your mother-in-law. What noises did you hear?" asked the chief.

"Love-making noises, Your Honour. You know, the kind of noises that men and women make in moments of physical intimacy. I could hear everything. And there was no way I could mistake Chigondo's voice. That is what happened."

"But what did you do when you realised that it was Chigondo in bed with your wife?" the chief asked.

"You all know what a strong man Chigondo is. Look at his muscles. I was angry but scared. So I waited until they finished their business and then I knocked on the door. They did not open it for a long time. When Chigondo finally came out, I told him that I knew what he had been doing."

"And what did he say?"

"Nothing. He just walked past me and said nothing. I then went inside and slapped my wife several times as she lay in bed. She kept on telling me that Chigondo had been trying to sell her some rabbits."

Everyone in the audience burst out laughing.

"Of course I did not believe her. That night I slept on the granary floor and I have not shared the mat with her since."

"Thank you, Matare. Now we must ask Chimhosva what happened," said the chief, as Matare sat down. Chimhosva stepped forward with a bemused look on her face.

"Do you know this man?" The chief pointed to Chigondo.

"Yes, I do. Everyone here knows Chigondo, the famous rabbit hunter," replied Chimhosva.

"Listen, Matare's wife, when I ask whether you 'know' this man, I mean do you know him more intimately than the rest of us do?"

Chimhosva looked around as if she was lost. Then she spotted one of her aunts in the audience and asked the chief if she could consult her relative on how to respond to the questions.

"You should have done that before you came here," Takesure said sternly.

Chimhosva stubbornly wiggled her bottom and walked over to her aunt. The older woman whispered into her ear for a couple of minutes and then Chimhosva returned to stand in front of Chief Matambo.

"Woman, you have not yet answered the question. Do you know this man?" the chief asked again.

"Excuse me a moment," Chimhosva said. Walking quickly, she disappeared behind the chief's house. After a brief moment she reappeared, this time with what seemed to be a piece of cream-coloured cloth in her hand. She walked slowly towards Chigondo and placed the cloth on his head. Then everyone realised that the 'cloth' on Chigondo's head was in fact an item of Chimhosva's underwear.

Everyone began to laugh. Slowly and calculatingly, Chimhosva picked up the underwear, slapped Chigondo's head with it and disappeared again. When she returned, Chief Matambo motioned to the audience to keep quiet.

"The woman has admitted that she knows Chigondo. No woman would have the courage to do what Chimhosva did unless she was absolutely certain that she had made love to the man. What do you say, Chigondo?"

Chigondo smiled, "Yes, Your Honour, as the woman herself has demonstrated, I do know Chimhosva. I know her in the same way that she knows me."

"But do you realise that knowing her the way you do is a crime?"

"Yes, Your Honour. As you can all see, the woman is beautiful. Just ask her to turn around and you can all see how well equipped she is. Not many women can boast of such a bottom. She was my childhood sweetheart. I should have married her." Some people laughed, but others muttered and called Chigondo a fool.

"The man admits his crime. Now, Matare, do you seek compensation from this man who has defiled your property. You paid *lobola* for Chimhosva did you not?"

"Yes, Chief. I paid five head of cattle, one goat and two hundred dollars. She was an expensive woman."

"When you paid your in-laws that much, it meant that you were buying exclusive rights to her body. Gentlemen, is that not correct?"

His advisers agreed in unison. But the women in the audience murmured in dissent.

"So, Matare, how much do you want to charge Chigondo for the crime?" asked Chief Matambo.

"Oh, I think . . . I think three cows and two goats will be all right."

Chigondo looked shocked. He complained that the charge was far too much. "After all, Chimhosva was not a virgin. Maybe Matare should also tell the court whether he still loves his wife or whether he does not want her any more. Because if he charges me that much, it means I can take her as my wife. Why should I pay so much for something that is not mine to keep?"

"What? Chigondo, what did you say?" A short, very dark-skinned woman came running up to Chigondo and grabbed his jacket. Simba told me that she was Chigondo's wife.

"So, you want to take Chimhosva as your wife? Have you gone out of your mind? Let me tell you that if you do that I will kill myself," she screamed.

"Order!" Takesure shouted. "Woman, go and sit down. You can talk about this with your husband when the court has finished with him."

Chigondo's wife gave Chimhosva an evil look and sat down right next to her. Chimhosva turned her head away and giggled.

"Matare, do you still want Chimhosva as your wife?"

"Yes, Your Honour," replied Matare. Some of the men jeered at him. As if addressing them, Matare said, "You might all think I am stupid, but you are wrong. I love my wife. We have six children and four grandchildren together. The compensation I have asked for will benefit the family and not just myself."

For the next few minutes, there were negotiations about the amount of compensation to be paid. Then the chief announced that Matare would be paid one cow and two goats. The people clapped their hands and the case was over. Chigondo's wife could be seen dragging him home while shouting that he was a useless husband.

"Case number two! Please be quick because our time is flying," called Takesure. Six solemn-looking people walked forward and sat down in front of the chief.

"Your Honour," Takesure began, "the people before you here are two married couples, one young man and a young girl who, as you can see, is pregnant. On my right hand are VaJoni and his wife, with their daughter Raina between them. On my left are VaMusendo and his wife, and standing next to them is their son Stephen. What has happened here is that Raina was in Form Four but has had to discontinue her education because she got pregnant. She claims that Stephen is responsible for her pregnancy. But Stephen says he is not sure that he is in fact responsible. VaJoni and his wife are here to claim compensation for the damage done to their daughter. That is the case in brief, Your Honour."

"How old are you?" the chief asked Raina.

"Seventeen."

"And you two are in love?"

"We were," replied Stephen.

"Then what happened?"

"She got pregnant."

"You made me pregnant!" shouted Raina.

"No, I did not!"

"I never had another boyfriend apart from you. Everyone can testify that the two of us walked home together from school every day," said Raina, bursting into tears.

"Where do these children go to school?" asked Chief Matambo.

"Saint Clara's High School," replied Raina's mother.

"But that is a long way away. It means these children have to cross two rivers to get there."

"Yes. That is how they find time and hide in the bushes to make babies," said Takesure.

"Do you admit that you slept with this girl?" the chief asked Stephen.

"Yes, but I did not mean to do it," he replied. "It only happened a couple of times. And there is no way I could have made her pregnant. I did biology at school, Your Honour, so I was careful and used the withdrawal method. Somebody else must have made her pregnant."

"Who?" asked the chief.

"Maybe it was the maths teacher. He does not take his eyes off her during lessons."

"So he made me pregnant with his eyes?" asked Raina.

"Maybe," said Stephen.

Within a split second, VaMusendo got up and slapped his son's face twice. "How dare you talk such rubbish! I work all night as a security guard in Harare, hoping that the little money I make will help me to educate my son. I guard rich people's houses at night and dream that one day I will walk past a security guard as I visit my educated boy's house. I can see that my dreams are futile. For all my hard work, all I get is a lazy boy who spends his time fornicating in the bushes on the way from school!" Stephen's father was shaking with rage.

"Calm down, VaMusendo. As fathers we all understand your anger," said Takesure.

"This is a simple case," said the chief. "Two young people are taught biology at school and on their way home, what do they do? They experiment – and a child is in the making. Stephen, do you want to marry this girl?"

Stephen's eyes were red with tears. "No," he said.

"Raina, do you want to marry Stephen?"

"Not now. Maybe one day."

Raina's mother looked at her daughter angrily. "Maybe one day. Maybe one day. Where will you be living till that one day comes? You chose to get pregnant, so you should go and live with the father of your child. We are not taking you home with us today."

"Now, woman, do not give the child a hard time," said VaJoni, turning to his wife. "It is all your fault. If this child had been given lessons on Christian behaviour and morality by you as her mother, she would not be pregnant. You do not care what happens to her. I actually think you encouraged her to get pregnant. You can take your daughter and leave my home. I will find another wife who knows how to bring up children."

"It is clear that these two young people are not ready to get married," said Chief Matambo. "When is the baby due, Raina?"

"In two months," said Raina sobbing.

"This is my ruling. Go home and wait till you deliver the baby, and then go back to school. Meanwhile, Stephen, continue your education until the baby is born. Then get a job and pay maintenance for your child. If you do not pay maintenance within three months after the child is born, we will summon you before this court and you will be charged. This will teach you not to eat the apple before you get enough teeth. All you do is mess it up. Do you understand?"

"Yes, Your Honour."

Turning to Raina's parents, the chief said, "One thing you must realise is that once a child is over fifteen, he or she can play around. The child that Raina is carrying is your child. You will have to look after it when it is born. Case complete."

Chief Matambo then rose to straighten his back. "Break time!" shouted Takesure. We were served *mahewu*, a homemade nonalcoholic drink made from maize porridge, yeast and sugar. Since there weren't enough cups to go round, I had to take turns with three elderly women in sipping from one mug. I couldn't help noticing that the woman who passed the mug on to me had teeth that were thickly stained brown – a sign that she took snuff by placing it under her tongue. I wondered when she had last used a stick to clean her teeth. Most villagers had never used toothbrushes or toothpaste; they simply could not afford such things. But village mothers taught their children traditional

135

teeth-cleaning methods. "Clean teeth are a measure of civilisation," my mother used to say. As children we used a *muchakata* stick or *mutokwiro* root to clean our teeth as we walked to school. The root was particularly effective because it made your lips bright red while leaving your teeth white. If there were stains we couldn't remove this way, we would find a piece of charcoal with which to scrub them clean.

"Case number three!" called Takesure, and I noticed what perfect teeth he had; he obviously used the traditional cleaning methods.

Three men and a group of women stood in front of the chief.

"Your Honour, what we have here is a case of witchcraft," said Takesure. "The woman who stands before you is Emma. The man next to her is Banda, the Malawian man who is her companion. Sir, for many years Emma worked in the cities as a comforter for lonely men. Her job was well paying, as is shown by the number of Western goods she brought home with her after the war. Since her return, Emma has been a good woman. But her relatives think that Banda is a witch and that he is responsible for some deaths that have recently occurred in the family."

I knew that Emma had left the village to get married years before. But her marriage had broken up because she could not have children, so she had gone to the city and become one of the first African prostitutes there. It was rumoured that she often slept with white men. I could remember her coming home at Christmas and wearing wigs and fashionable Western clothes in the village. She would put on a glamorous dress, a hat and a pair of white gloves; then, shielding herself from the sun with a white parasol, she would take a walk along the road wishing everyone she met the compliments of the season.

One day after the war, Emma came home with a Malawian

man who hardly spoke Shona. They arrived in a hired truck full of radios, wardrobes, beds, cupboards and any number of clothes. Their affluence became the talk of the village. Within a few months, Emma and Banda had built themselves two grass-thatched huts which served them as bedroom and kitchen. The pair were almost inseparable, but what surprised most people was that Banda did all the housework and other jobs normally reserved for women: he worked in the fields, cooked, sewed and fetched water. At beer parties, Emma would order Banda to go home before sunset and prepare dinner and Banda would do as he was told without complaining.

When people asked Emma why she had decided to leave the city after so many years she had an explanation ready. "After independence the competition for men in Harare bars became very tough. Men prefer younger women, so I thought that it was time for me to come home and start another life. I was lucky to get a man I could bring home. Banda is quite happy to be my 'wife'."

Being the senior aunt in her large extended family, Emma was often consulted by her brothers on family issues. She played a powerful, matriarchal role, even advising her brothers on how to discipline their wives. Her elevation to this position was not easily accepted by several of the village women, particularly her sisters-in-law. After the deaths of some children in the extended family, the women decided to consult a *n'anga*, who told them that a foreigner from somewhere far away had brought an evil spirit into the family. He urged them to send the foreigner away before he 'ate' all the children in the family.

"My twins died last year," said one of Emma's sisters-in-law to the chief. "Now my son has got incurable tuberculosis. This is not bad luck. We all know that the foreigner responsible for our misfortunes is Banda."

"Whoever heard of a man who behaves like a woman?" said one of Emma's cousins. "This Malawian is not normal. He is possessed by the spirit of a female witch who devours children. He must leave our village."

Banda was a short man with bow legs. His grey hair was neatly cut and combed, and he wore a suit and tie and shiny black shoes. In comparison to most of the villagers, he looked very smart and urban. He sat on a stool next to Emma, who was standing, and held her hand. She looked more like the little man's big-bosomed mother than his mistress. She kept on whispering to him in Chichewa, a Malawian language which no-one else could understand.

"So is the Malawian the cause for this gathering?" asked the chief.

"Yes, Your Honour. We want him to leave our village as soon as possible," another of Emma's female relatives said. "We all know that when he goes, our family will enjoy peace and good health." The other members of Emma's family agreed unanimously.

Chief Matambo and his advisers discussed the case in low tones. Banda smoked his pipe silently while Emma gently massaged his neck.

Finally, the chief said, "Emma, I feel that for the sake of peace in your extended family, Banda must return to his own country."

Emma and Banda shook their heads in sad resignation. Then Emma asked for permission to speak: "Your Honour, I stand before you with great disillusionment. How can my own family be so jealous of me? I do not have children of my own, but for years I have educated my brothers' children. I have also clothed my brothers and their wives. Banda did all the odd jobs for the family and he never crossed words with anyone. I cannot believe that my family now wants to get rid of Banda. And how can Your Honour be so uncivilised as to believe in their witchcraft rubbish? Who does not know that my sister-in-law's twins died of measles because they were not immunised against it? Who also does not know that tuberculosis or pneumonia means a person has got AIDS?

"But I realise I cannot change the minds of ignorant, primitive people. For this reason, I shall return to the city with Banda and I will never come back here again. Please grant us two weeks to get ourselves organised."

As soon as Emma finished speaking, her relatives started arguing among themselves. One faction pointed out that if Emma went to the city, their families would starve because they relied on her to supplement their food during periods of drought. But another group maintained that her absence would rid them of many evils to come.

Emma told them not to argue among themselves, as she had already made up her mind not to live among 'uncivilised savages'. Demonstrating a physical intimacy not often seen in public, she took Banda's arm and they walked away.

The chief laughed: "Ah, that Emma is a law unto herself. No-one can ever dream of controlling her. Lucky she has a 'wife' to look after her."

"Case number four!" shouted Takesure.

I stepped forward, followed by Simba. Amosi joined us and we all stood in front of the chief. Takesure explained the case to the chief, who kept on nodding his head. He interrupted the policeman at one point to ask what spaghetti was.

"Wormlike things that white people eat," replied Simba.

"Where is this bedspread?" asked the chief, when Takesure

had finished.

"It has been cut into several pieces in order to sew children's dresses," I said.

"Amosi, your wife is a fool," said Chief Matambo. "How could she make clothes from this bedspread? Did it not occur to her that someone was bound to realise that the material had been stolen?"

"The woman did not know that the bedspread had been stolen from a house nearby," said Simba.

"This is an easy case. How much did the bedspread cost?"

I had to think for a while. "I got it as a birthday present from my mother-in-law. She bought it in Bali for something like fifty US dollars."

"How much?"

"Fifty dollars from America," said Takesure. "Your Honour, I forgot to tell you. The woman who stands humbly in front of you is a typical example of what education should do for our people. This is Teacher David's daughter. She has been to countries where the white people live."

I was getting quite self-conscious and embarrassed, but Takesure continued. "This woman has swallowed books and speaks English as if she was born in England. She even married a white man. But she knows where she comes from, unlike the young people from this village who go to Harare and Bulawayo and then come back claiming not to speak our language."

"Oh, young lady!" said Chief Matambo. "I knew your father very well. But David had many daughters – which number are you in the family?"

"Seven," I said.

"Next time you come here, do bring me a bottle of whisky and some cigarettes," said the chief. Then, turning to Amosi, he said, "Pay back the price of the bedspread."

"But I cannot afford to pay for it, Your Honour. Fifty US dollars is a lot of money – more than four hundred Zimbabwean dollars! Where would I get it?"

"If you do not have the money, pay the charge with some goats."

"Goats cost about eighty dollars each. So this means I would have to pay about five goats just for a bedspread. Sir, have mercy on me."

I knew that Amosi could not pay even one goat. Then an idea occurred to me. "Your Honour, since Amosi is a very strong man, may I suggest that he make a thousand bricks for the school as a contribution towards the new building? I accept that I have lost my bedspread, but at least some children will have benefited from it if Amosi does this work and is not paid for his labour."

"The case is settled," said the chief. Amosi looked horrified as he walked away from the court.

It was already two o'clock in the afternoon and I told Simba that we should begin our long walk home.

"But don't you want to stay for case number five?" he asked.

"No, not really. What is it about?" I asked, only half-interested.

"It is about a rape. Everyone knows about this case," Simba said.

"You tell me about it as we walk home," I suggested, and so we left the court.

"Have you heard of Nyika?" asked Simba, as we walked.

"No."

"He is about sixty years old. His sister and her husband died in the war and left several children in his care. The youngest child was one year old at the time. Now she is sixteen and the dirty old man has been raping her for years."

"That's shocking," I said. "How did people know about it?"

"She got pregnant, didn't she? So Nyika's wife has brought him to court. I think Nyika ought to go to prison."

"But can the chief sentence people to prison?" I asked.

"No. Serious cases like rape or murder can no longer be handled by a chief. It is Chief Matambo's responsibility to report the case to the nearest police station. Tomorrow Takesure will go and alert the police and they will send a car down here. Rape is regarded as a serious matter," said Simba.

After a pause, he continued, "If a girl says to me that she is not interested in sex, I do not push her. There are many older women who are interested. If I cannot get a young girl, I can always go after older women. Nyika will go to prison for sure."

"But he is so old. I think they will give him a lenient sentence," I said.

"When he comes back from prison, he will have to pay a number of cattle to his niece's relatives. In the past, I am told that it was easy to get away with rape and even incest, but not these days. After independence the black government wants to protect women. Sometimes they overdo it, though."

I was too tired to argue the point with Simba. He chatted all the way home while I listened in silence.

▰▰▰

As we approached the homestead, we saw a terribly skinny man dressed in dirty old rags, his hair in dreadlocks, walking away in the opposite direction. When we went into the house, I asked my mother who he was.

"That is Samson," she replied. "He is a madman, just like his uncle and his grandfather."

I recalled having seen Samson once before, at the village shopping centre. He was talking to himself and begging for food. Everyone fed him, because refusing to feed a madman was believed to bring bad luck.

"The reason Samson's grandfather went mad was because he committed two crimes against his mother," remarked Christmas. "He insulted her by calling her a whore and then he slapped her face. That was a great crime."

Mothers are traditionally regarded as sacred in Shona culture. You can easily get away with assaulting your father but never your mother. If you have committed a crime against your mother, you must prove that you are genuinely sorry by performing specified cleansing rituals.

"You remember how Jaison's father assaulted his mother one year? She died before she had forgiven him and he was forced to perform the rites," Amai said.

"He probably did not do it properly," said Christmas. "Look at Jaison, he is still not quite normal."

One day, about twenty years ago, several of us children were playing in the front yard at our homestead when a man wearing sackcloth and covered in ashes came through the gate. He headed straight for the rubbish pit and sat down beside it. It was only after some time that we realised this was Nhau, Jaison's father.

Amai and Maiguru, who had come out of the house, stared at the newcomer for a while; then they started pointing at him and jeering. They threw sticks at him and Maiguru poured handfuls of ashes from the fireplace on his head.

"The fool who dared insult his mother!" jeered Amai.

"Who bore nine months of pregnancy and went through hours of labour pains?" asked Maiguru. "Was it not your mother?"

"Then who breast-fed you until you were able to chew your own food? Who spent so many sleepless nights when you suffered from measles and other childhood illnesses? Was it not your mother?"

Turning to us children, Maiguru asked us to gather some corn husks and string them together like a necklace. She took the necklace we made and tied it around Nhau's neck. Amai spat and threw pebbles at him.

"Nhau, the son who should have been left outside at birth for the jackals to eat," Maiguru jeered.

Then Amai took a plate of cold *sadza* left over from the previous night and placed it in the dust next to Nhau, who clapped his hands and smiled the way mad beggars do. Maiguru rushed into the kitchen and brought out some salted water: "Here is some sauce for your *sadza*." Nhau dipped morsels of *sadza* in the salted water and started eating it hurriedly. We all laughed at the way he grimaced and swallowed the food with evident distaste.

"Beggar, what do you have in your sack?" Amai asked, when Nhau had finished eating. Nhau opened the sack that he had been carrying over his shoulder. Silently, he showed Amai the sorghum he had collected from other people. Amai went into the granary and brought back a potful of sorghum which she poured into the sack. Nhau knelt down and clapped his hands in gratitude. As he walked away, Amai and Maiguru threw more ashes at him and kept on jeering.

At the next village Nhau would get the same treatment. For two weeks he begged for grain in this way until he had ten buckets of sorghum and three buckets of maize. Then for two days he ground the sorghum – woman's work, which he did without any assistance. Then he prepared three drums of beer and told the elders of his village that he was ready for the final cleansing ceremony.

All the people in the village were invited to attend. As part of the ceremony, an ox was killed and its meat consumed without salt; eating saltless meat was a way of participating in Nhau's suffering. Then Nhau begged his mother's spirit for forgiveness. If he had not performed the cleansing rituals, his mother's spirit would have haunted him and his children for many years to come. It was a lesson to all those who dared insult their mothers.

"Ah, but for people living in the cities, none of that matters any more," said Sydney. "Have you not heard about mothers who are forced to live in the servants' quarters because their sons do not have enough room to keep them? Mothers are being insulted by their sons and their sons' wives day in day out in the cities."

"Cleansing ceremonies do not work in the city," said Christmas. "They only work in the village. But it does not matter where you live: if you insult your mother, bad luck will follow you."

CHAPTER 9

Harare Parties

THIS WEEKEND we are not going to the village, as Adam has some urgent film footage that needs to be edited in Harare. Saturday mornings in the city are lazy and slow. After a big breakfast of sausages, bacon and fried eggs, we go out onto the verandah for a cup of coffee. There are two types of coffee in Zimbabwe – instant and the real stuff grown in the Eastern Highlands, mainly for export.

I flip through the thin newspaper, searching for the entertainment page. Apart from films that we have already seen on video in Australia, there is very little on offer in Harare. Two makeshift theatres stage dreadful amateur versions of Andrew Lloyd Webber musicals, which are of little interest to most black Zimbabweans; there is a strong belief among the locals that only white people go to these performances. This could be a legacy of the colonial past. Before independence, live theatre was mainly for whites only; at the cinema, black people often had to be content with the cheaper seats close to the screen, while white people sat further back or in the balcony area.

Since independence things have changed: people can sit wherever they like in the cinema and the more enlightened members of the expatriate community have tried hard to encourage indigenous theatre. However, very few black Zimbabweans attend live performances of any kind; the idea of paying to see someone act is still foreign to a majority of black people. And as for classical concerts with symphony orchestras and slow, soft music, they are a recipe for boredom. Where is the beer and dancing?

I resign myself to an uneventful Saturday afternoon. Viola, our housekeeper, has written a short list of grocery shopping that needs to be done, so I head off to the supermarket. I enjoy shopping here because I can buy virtually everything I want: South African Weetbix, New Zealand lemon grass, tinned British oysters, and various beers and wines from all over the world. By Zimbabwean standards most of the imported goods are pretty expensive, but for 'expatriates' like Adam and me, life is not too costly. I can easily cook a Thai or Indian dish using all the ingredients I used to buy in Melbourne, and it only costs me about half the price here. The secret is knowing where to get exotic foodstuffs – authentic curry powders, good soy sauce or fresh coriander. I have been living in Harare long enough to know where to find these things, and this is one of those times when I want to be creative in the kitchen in order to ease the tedium of the day.

As I try to prevent Jack from grabbing everything he sees on the supermarket shelves, I become aware that a woman standing in the same aisle is watching me. Her face is very familiar but I cannot remember whether I went to boarding school or nursing college with her. Then she greets me, calling me by my name and shaking my hand strongly, and I recognise her voice immediately. Margaret Khumalo, one of the Zimbabwean girls I used to know in London fifteen years ago. Once I have placed her, her face brings back a tide of memories.

"You have not changed much," I say.

"Nor have you. Except for the hair. So what is this hairstyle? Gone Rastafarian have you?" says Margaret, laughing.

"No. I could not get anyone to plait it when I was in Melbourne. It was a lot cheaper and easier to go natural."

We talk about the past, in English; Margaret speaks rather loudly. While shoppers walk past us with their trolleys, she tells me that she is divorced and has two children. She returned to Harare in 1987 and is now teaching sociology at the University of Zimbabwe.

After we exchange telephone numbers, Margaret says, "You see all these groceries I have bought?"

Her trolley is full of snacks, sausages, bread, dozens of cans of beer and a few bottles of wine.

"Are you having a party or something?"

"Yes. You must come. It is my sister-in-law's baby shower this afternoon. Have you got anything planned?"

"Not really – I might come. Just give me the address."

She scribbles the address on the back of her business card. "The party is at my sister-in-law's friend's place. It will be a scream. Bring a friend. Anyone is welcome as long as it is not a man – this is a women-only party!"

"What time does it start?"

"Any time after two. You know, African time. See you later!" And she wheels her heavy trolley to the till.

I cannot get over seeing Margaret after so many years. Coincidentally, our first meeting also took place in a supermarket: the Safeway near Russell Square in London. Margaret had grown up in Bulawayo; of Ndebele stock, she hardly spoke Shona. She was doing her undergraduate degree in anthropology at the

School of Oriental and African Studies while I was studying for a nursing diploma in child health at Great Ormond Street children's hospital. I would have liked to be Margaret's friend, but I was disappointed that we had to communicate in English although we came from the same country. Whenever I met black women in London I felt let down if they did not speak Shona.

So at the start, I deliberately kept my distance from Margaret. In retrospect, I realise that my attitude towards her reflected my jealousy of her fluent English. At the time, I spoke the English of Methodist Missionaries, and my accent was very much influenced by Shona. Margaret had gone to a multi-racial school in Rhodesia and so her English was faultless.

Although I gradually became friends with Margaret, I still envied her for being beautiful, intelligent, privileged, outspoken and wild. It did not matter to her whether a man was Italian, Greek, West Indian, English or Swedish – she went out with different men all the time. I could never keep up with her love life. Her various boyfriends used to turn up at my place at odd hours looking for her.

Then one day Margaret invited me to her engagement party. She had met her fiancé only a few months before. Jonathan, the son of a Zimbabwean diplomat, was tall, strong and extremely handsome, and he absolutely adored Margaret. I became more and more envious: that girl had everything and now she was going to marry a Shona even though she was Ndebele. Naively, I wondered why she had to deprive someone like me of a good Shona man.

When I get home from the supermarket, Viola tells me that Kim from the Australian High Commission called. Kim and I were at university together in Melbourne. Now she is Third Secretary at the high commission and we occasionally meet for coffee. I dial her number.

"Just wondering whether you wanted to have coffee at the Italian bakery in Avondale," says Kim. "Mandy is coming too." Mandy is head of the aid section at the high commission.

"I would have loved to, but I have been invited to a baby shower this afternoon."

"Baby shower? What's that?"

"I have never been to one but I understand that it is a party for women only. They drink and talk about babies."

"Urgh – charming stuff." Kim is single and not particularly baby-oriented.

"It could be fun. Why don't you and Mandy come with me? We will just drop in for a little while. If there is too much talk about nappies and breast milk, we will go off and have a cappuccino and some cakes instead."

"I'll see what Mandy thinks, and call you back." Five minutes later, she rings to say that Mandy has heard so much about baby showers in Zimbabwe that she would be delighted to go. Kim has been persuaded to attend as well.

So the three of us arrive at the address Margaret gave me just after 3 p.m. There is hardly anyone there. Margaret wears jeans under a wraparound cloth as she rushes around putting the final touches to vast amounts of food laid out on a big table in the garden.

"Excuse the mess," she says in passing. "Please do have a drink and make yourselves comfortable." We join a couple of women sitting in the shade. We are obviously too early: three or four women are still frantically arranging and rearranging hired chairs while two young men are giving instructions to another woman on how to operate the music system.

Margaret opens a bottle of French champagne and offers it to us. "A gift from someone at the French Embassy."

Eventually, in twos, threes or even fives, the guests start arriving. Each woman carries bottles of wine or beer and a present; the smaller gifts are wrapped in a nappy.

"We did not bring a present. This is embarrassing," says Kim.

"Margaret didn't tell me to bring one," I say.

"Where is the sister-in-law who is having a baby?" asks Mandy.

One of the guests overhears the question. "She is getting dressed. She will be out as soon as those two young men leave."

The guests keep on arriving. Some are driving very expensive cars, others have walked from the bus stop and others have been dropped off outside the gate by their husbands or partners. One woman, who later identifies herself as 'Rita, the master of ceremonies at baby showers and kitchen parties', arrives wearing a long skirt; she is accompanied by two friends who are wearing knee-length dresses. Before sitting down, Rita and her friends take off their demure dresses and reveal the sexy clothing they have on underneath.

"What do you think of this?" Rita says, showing off her micro miniskirt and tight T-shirt.

"You ain't seen nothing yet," say her two friends, as they parade themselves in bicycle shorts.

"My husband would kill me if he were to see this skirt," laughs Rita.

As the party warms up, the sheer openness among these women takes me by surprise. They talk frankly about their personal lives, and discuss their relationships with their husbands as if the husbands were just people they happened to know. It is also interesting to see that whether a woman is Shona or Ndebele seems to make no difference; some of them speak both languages, and English as well.

"Does your husband know you drink beer?" Rita asks one of the guests, a woman called Thandie.

"No, no. Never. As far as my husband and your husband know, women drink only fruit punch, Coke, lemonade and other innocent, nonalcoholic drinks at baby showers."

"Rubbish," says Rita. "Most men now know that we drink beer. Ask Tiyekile, she will tell you what her husband thinks of baby showers. Where is she?"

"She has been doing some artwork on the mother-to-be. Here she comes."

Tiyekile, a big, light-skinned woman, is a cousin of Margaret's. "Tiye, tell them what your husband thinks of baby showers and kitchen parties."

Tiyekile takes a big swig from a beer bottle and smiles. Then she lifts up her skirt to reveal a huge black bruise on one of her thighs. "A golf club did this," she says, with a raucous laugh.

"Tell the others what happened," says Thandie.

"Well, ladies, for quite some time I have been telling my husband that I go to baby showers on Saturdays. Like all men, at weekends he goes off to drink or to see his girlfriend, and he did not seem to mind my going to women's parties. Twice he came home earlier than I did but he did not complain that I was not there. Then someone from his work told him that baby showers or kitchen parties are not innocent events. 'Zimbabwean women have learnt how to make love to each other,' this man said. My husband came home and told me that I was not to attend these parties any more. But I did – and I got a real bashing."

Tiyekile sits down and keeps drinking.

"So how come you are here?" asks someone.

"Because I will not let a man deprive me of the only form of entertainment I can get," replies Tiyekile. "When he goes out to drink three times a week and spends money on women, do I stop him?"

"No – let him drink and let him prostitute himself," agrees Chipo. "You just carry on with your life. If he keeps beating you, leave him. I left mine and I do not regret it at all."

"It is not that easy to leave a man," remarks Agnes. "If you leave him, you lose the house, your family breaks up and you become destitute."

"Not any more," says Chipo. "If you are a professional woman, like most of us here, you just get a good lawyer to represent you. All you need is firm evidence that he is a useless bastard."

"But we are not all professional women," says Agnes. "I make a living from sewing bedspreads and working as a secretary. My salary alone could never be enough for the mortgage."

"But you have a good husband," says Tiyekile.

"What do you mean? You mean he is good because he does not beat me up. Don't you realise that he cannot afford to beat me? If he does, I will stop cooking for his mother, his brother, his cousin, his nephew and all his relatives who seem to think that our house is a hotel."

The discussion goes on. The two men who have been setting up the sound system take their leave, and a female disc jockey starts playing music. Peanuts and chips are being passed round by a couple of waitresses. There must be about fifty to sixty women present.

"Here she comes!" shouts Rita. "At last the great mother

herself appears."

A heavily pregnant woman in her early thirties walks steadily out of the house and approaches the guests. Apart from a pair of lacy knickers and a bra, she is wearing nothing. Her abdomen and face have been painted with coloured designs. Some of the drawings on her stomach are almost pornographic. Margaret spreads a beautiful cloth on the ground and helps her sister-in-law to sit down.

"Introductions! Introductions first before we can get into the full swing of the party!" cries Rita. "Let us start with you." She points at Agnes.

"My name is Virgins Do Not Cry," says Agnes and everyone bursts out laughing.

"My name is Beautiful Breasts," says Tiyekile, shaking her big bust at everyone.

"And I am Ms Big Bottoms Are Sexy," says another guest, shaking her bottom.

The introductions go on around the circle of women and everyone identifies themselves with sexually suggestive names.

When it is my turn, I get up and say, "My name is I Need To Know More."

For a moment, the other women look puzzled. "What do you need to know that your aunt or good books have not taught you?" asks Rita. I realise that the name I have chosen is not exciting enough and I quickly sit down.

"My name is Women Unite," says Kim.

"We are united already! How united do you want us to be? Look!" says Thandie, hugging Agnes and kissing her on the cheek. Tiyekile gets up and kisses Agnes on the other cheek. Everyone is laughing.

"And my name is . . . Oh, I cannot think – this is too

embarrassing!" Mandy sits down, blushing. The women laugh in sympathy, and Margaret places her hand on Mandy's shoulder and tells her not to worry.

"Ladies, my name is Rita, and as you know I am the MC at most good baby showers and kitchen parties. The lady sitting on the ground with a huge tummy is Verona. Verona tasted the good apple and see what happened to her – she is eight months pregnant. In one month she will experience the pain prescribed for all women – the pain of labour. This is her first child, so she really is a novice to this business and she will have to learn that delivering a baby is not child's play. Over here on my right is Verona's sister-in-law, Margaret. Margaret has taken her responsibilities as a sister-in-law seriously. As you can see, she has provided plenty of food and plenty of alcohol for everyone. Now, let us begin our party by opening the presents."

Next to Verona are piles and piles of presents. Verona picks up a parcel wrapped in a nappy, feels it carefully and announces that there are two feeding bottles inside. The present is unwrapped: Verona's guess was right. The two bottles are held up for everyone to see and Rita asks who brought them. One of the women puts up her hand and everyone claps.

The guessing game continues. The smaller presents are easy to identify correctly because Verona can feel the contents through the nappies. For a while she does well, guessing all the contents correctly, until she comes to Margaret's gift, a huge box concealed in wrapping paper. Then, although she tries as hard as she can, Verona fails to guess what it contains.

"Punishment! Punishment!" the women shout. "Verona must dance!"

"All right!" says Rita. "What music do you want to dance to, Verona?"

"Kanda Bongo's *kwasa-kwasa*," says Verona.

"*Kwasa-kwasa* is the name for any Zairean music. Which particular piece by Kanda Bongo?"

"Choose 'Isambe'!" shouts the DJ.

Everyone sits down except for Verona, who stands in the middle of the circle. When the music begins, she starts moving her whole body slowly from left to right. Then she shakes her fingers and knees rhythmically. As the music gets faster, she lifts one leg and thrusts her pelvis back and forth, up and down. Pausing for a second, she rolls her eyes, sticks her tongue out and seductively licks her lips and her fingers. Then, standing quite still, she tilts her head a little bit and moves only her thighs and bottom.

The women clap their hands in uproarious appreciation. "Ah! She can still do it! She can still do it!"

"Why not?" says an older woman. "Pregnancy is not an illness."

When the song finishes Verona sits down, sweating. Margaret produces a damp towel and wipes her sister-in-law's face.

"Now that you have been punished, you can open the present," says Rita. Verona slowly unwraps the huge parcel and everyone claps again as a British Mothercare pram is revealed.

"For my long-awaited niece or nephew," says Margaret proudly. Verona hugs her and kisses her on the cheek. There is more clapping and some of the guests dance and ululate the way village women do.

"Educated women certainly look after themselves," says Agnes sadly. "That pram must have cost at least two thousand dollars. If Verona had her baby ten years ago, like some of us did, she probably would not have got all these presents."

"Professional women have babies when they know that they

are ready and that they can afford them," says Thandie. "Margaret had her children after she got her Master's degree and Verona completed her doctorate last year. Now she is ready for motherhood."

"Unless you have got plenty of money, there is no need to rush into having babies these days," says Agnes. "I do wish I had finished high school before getting pregnant."

Meanwhile, Verona keeps opening her gifts. Whenever she fails to guess correctly, she asks one of her friends to dance in punishment for her as she is too tired.

After all the presents have been opened, it is time to eat. I take the opportunity to talk to various women; they tell me about unfaithful husbands, difficult mothers-in-law, the high cost of living. I discover that most of the women, who are aged between twenty and forty-five, have been married at some time; but a good number of them are now widowed, separated or divorced. They are mostly urban, middle-class women who, like me, have studied abroad and benefited from Zimbabwean independence; among them are lawyers, doctors, nurses, teachers and self-employed businesswomen. Many of them have a rural background like mine. They talk about their mothers and mothers-in-law, who still live in their villages; these women only go back there occasionally – for a funeral, for instance.

In comparison to their Western counterparts, these women's lives are quite comfortable. Most of them have a full-time housekeeper, nanny or gardener. After independence, black couples who had a bit of money could easily afford houses in the former whites-only suburbs, and the majority of women at this party have houses set on one or two acres, complete with swimming pool and tennis court. Their children attend private schools and go on to university, either here or overseas. They are a new generation of professional Zimbabwean women who have only tenuous ties to traditional village culture.

After we have eaten, Rita calls for more music. The DJ begins playing popular South African tunes. The guests are scattered all over the garden and they dance wherever they happen to be standing. Every now and again a circle forms, and one woman dances in the middle. Another one joins her and the two dance together, acting out male and female roles respectively. The female dancer seductively wiggles her bottom at her partner while 'he' thrusts 'his' pelvis at her.

Mandy, Kim and I join in the dancing. At one stage I notice that Kim is dancing with two 'men' and seems to be thoroughly enjoying every minute of it. Mandy is keeping her distance from this trio, as if fearing that she might be invited to participate in what appears to be simulated sex.

When the music ends, the DJ sits down and relaxes. Rita takes the microphone and announces that it is time for some serious lessons on childbirth and baby care. The women settle them- selves calmly − it is difficult to believe that they have been dancing wildly only a few minutes before.

A guest who identifies herself as a mid-wife and a community health nurse stands up and starts talking. For a good fifteen minutes, she speaks about the last stages of pregnancy, how to recognise labour pains, what to do and when to get to hospital, the labour itself, breast-feeding and postnatal care. Verona then has the chance to express her fears and ask the mid-wife ques- tions, which she answers sensitively. Other women offer Verona advice based on their own experiences of childbirth and moth- erhood.

"Stay away from commercial powdered milk as much as you can," says the mid-wife. "Gone are the days when we thought

Nestlé was better than breast milk." She goes on to describe how a nursing mother should care for her breasts and warns Verona to keep up her personal hygiene. "Do not think that because you are now a mother, you do not have to look attractive."

"If you neglect yourself, your husband will run away," says one of the women.

"Sometimes a husband will look at his wife's breasts oozing milk and think 'Yuk'!" says Thandie. "Then he will go looking for schoolgirls with firm breasts."

"Who cares? Once I have my baby, why should I want to have sex so soon?" someone asks.

"But ladies," says the mid-wife, "your husband should be your number one priority. The baby comes second."

"What a ridiculous idea," Kim whispers to me. "He should be the one looking after you – not the other way round."

"I did my best for my husband after my first child was born," says a woman. "But nothing worked. He actually left me for another woman when the baby was six weeks old."

"But not all men are like that," says someone else. "The husband of a friend of mine actually stopped drinking and came straight home after work every day so he could play with the baby. The child is now five years old and absolutely adores his dad."

"Enough of husbands!" chips in Rita. Turning to the mid-wife she asks, "Sister, is there anything you want to add to a very informative lesson which we have all greatly appreciated?"

"I just want Verona to know that she can call me at any time if she needs help." The mid-wife sits down and the guests ululate and clap their hands.

"So baby showers are not just booze and fun," observes Mandy.

I explain that baby showers fulfil a function that used to be taken care of by a woman's aunts. According to village tradition, a young girl first learnt about sex from her father's sister or from older girls in the village. During pregnancy, a village woman relied on close members of her extended family to give her medicine that would prepare her cervix for dilation during childbirth, and after the baby was born, these older women were always available to offer the woman any support she needed. But that was life in the village. Like me, the urban women at this party have spent most of their teenage years in mission boarding schools and missed out on traditional lore about childbirth. And living in Harare these days, they lack support from their village in-laws. They have to rely on close friends or attend baby showers to learn about pregnancy and childbirth. Similarly, at kitchen parties, held two weeks before a wedding, the bride receives presents for her new home as well as advice on married life.

"Now the serious part of the business is over. Back to the music!" shouts Rita. The dancing starts up again. Verona has got dressed and joins in. The sun has gone down and the party is getting wilder and wilder.

"Some of the dancing is almost like foreplay," says Mandy. "Do you think some of these women could be lesbians?"

I knew Mandy was going to ask me this question. I cannot say that there are no lesbians in Zimbabwe; although homosexuality is regarded as a crime, of course this does not mean that it does not exist. But it is just not acknowledged openly, unlike in the Western world. Some people argue that lesbians are more easily tolerated than gays because Zimbabwean men do not really care what two women do with each other. But then again, everyone knows that for two consecutive years the President of Zimbabwe has condemned a display of gay and lesbian material at the international book fair held in Harare.

Mandy's question reminds me of my sister Vongai, who worked at a women's refuge in Melbourne run by a group of lesbians. She maintained that she got the job there because they wanted to be seen as being fair to women from Non-English-Speaking Backgrounds.

"But you are not a lesbian," my sister Jessie said, when Vongai told us about her new job.

"It does not matter. I can be forgiven for my sexual preferences since I am the politically correct colour," replied Vongai.

Although Vongai continued to argue that lesbian politics did not influence her, after a few months we all noticed that she was dressing differently. One day all the women in the family got together to talk to her about the way she was dressing, hoping to deter her from going down the same path as her lesbian workmates.

"You are wearing heavy boots," said Jessie, when Vongai came over for the dinner-party we had planned.

"So what? They are comfortable," Vongai replied.

"How about shaving your head on both sides and leaving a pony tail at the back?" We all laughed.

"My dreadlocks are just fine."

"Would you care for a pork chop? Oh, sorry – I forgot that you have not only become pro-lesbian but are now a vegetarian as well," said Jessie.

"You are an African woman," said our cousin Mai Nina. She was older than the rest of us and we respected her. "African women should be proud of what they are. Why are you imitating these men-hating separatist lesbians who collect sperm in test tubes if they want to have babies?"

At this stage, everyone looked at me for a comment. I was regarded as the one who knew most about the ways of Westerners. I simply shrugged my shoulders, wishing that I was not part of the conversation. "Vongai can do what she likes. If she wants to be a vegetarian and to wear heavy boots, that is her business."

"Oh, tell the truth!" said Mai Nina. "Would you be comfortable taking Vongai to the village dressed as she is?" The question was directed at me.

"Look, I dress this way because I like it, not because I am a lesbian," said Vongai. "I am not one and I do not intend to be one. If any one of you here finds a thoughtful, sensitive and good-looking man, bring him to me – I will take good care of him."

"There are not many around," admitted Jessie, smiling.

"I think I will go back home and find a village boy," said Vongai. "I will educate him, send him to the gym, teach him to eat vegetables and to become a yuppy!"

The conversation ended in general laughter, although the rest of us secretly thought that if Vongai stayed at the women's refuge, she would become a lesbian.

Meanwhile, Mandy is still waiting for my answer. "These women do not sleep together," I say. "But in African society it can be difficult to define a lesbian. I know many women who maintain long-term friendships with other women which are not based on any sexual intimacy. The majority of these women have never heard of lesbianism, yet they are often closer to other women than to anyone else – even their husbands. In the village, for instance, it is quite usual for a woman to live without a man for long periods while her husband works in the city. At times, you see women like this holding hands with each other in public or even sharing a bed. So you see, it is difficult to answer your question."

"Absolutely fascinating," Mandy says, jiggling her keys. "I don't think Kim is ready to go yet, but do you mind if I leave now?"

"Not at all," I reply as I allow a 'male' dancer to whisk me away.

But after just one wild dance, Joyce, my partner, says regretfully that it is time she left too.

"So soon?" I say. "It is only 7 p.m."

"I am not going home yet. You see, I promised my boyfriend that I would meet him for a drink at seven. I told my husband that I would be back by nine. I have two hours to be with my lover. So let me disappear."

"What if your husband comes by looking for you?" asks Rita, who has overheard her.

"Tell him that I have gone to the funeral of a colleague's relative."

"But the way you are dressed will give you away when you get home," I say.

Joyce laughs. "I am not new to this game. I have my black scarf and wraparound cloth in the car, just in case my husband gets home before I do. See you later." And off she goes.

But less than an hour later, Joyce is back at the party.

"What happened?" asks Rita.

"Well, I saw my boyfriend but we did not have enough time to do anything. Ah, married men are a nuisance!"

"Why?"

"He had to get back home quickly because his wife's grandmother died in her village. Imagine, he actually left his wife crying so that he could see me briefly."

"But what did he say to his wife when he went out?" I ask.

"I don't know – some lie," replies Joyce.

"Rubbish! He has probably gone to see another girlfriend," says Rita. "How can you prove that his wife's grandmother died unless you ask the wife? He lied to you."

"I do not think so. I have been going out with this guy for three years. He does not lie to me."

"There is always a first time!"

"Oh, do not be so cruel," I say.

"Cruel? It is men who are cruel. The truth is that women do not want to believe it," says Rita, swaying her hips slowly. "But what does it matter anyway? Joyce is cheating on her husband, her boyfriend is cheating on his wife and Joyce's husband is cheating on her. So the circle of unfaithfulness goes on."

"But let us be fair. I only started cheating on my husband when I discovered that he has a child with another woman. It was tit for tat," says Joyce.

Kim and some other women have joined us, taking a break from their dancing. "I am glad that I do not have to cheat anyone," remarks one of them, a woman called Mary.

"Do you have a good husband?" asks Kim.

"No. He is dead."

"Oh, I am sorry. What did he die from? An accident?" asks Kim.

"No. He just became very ill," replies Mary.

"Tell your white friend that people do not ask questions like that any more," a woman whispers in Shona to me.

"When did your husband die?" someone else asks Mary.

"Oh, about three years ago."

"In that case," says the woman, who has kept on wiggling her bottom slowly in time to the music, "in that case you are a junior widow. My husband died five years ago so I am the senior widow!"

Everyone laughs. But the woman next to me goes on whispering. "AIDS is what is making widows of so many of these young women. My own husband died two years ago. But why should I worry about it? At the moment I am quite healthy. People say to me, go and get yourself tested. What for? If I find that I am HIV positive, what do I do? Kill myself? I want to enjoy life and dance! If AIDS catches up with me, I would at least have tried to be happy." She places her arm gently around my shoulders.

"Excuse me! Excuse me! Silence please!" shouts Rita, who is now visibly drunk. She is staggering towards the microphone but Margaret, who has been busy looking after the guests, grabs it before Rita can get there.

"Excuse us, ladies, we have made one mistake. Since we started this party, we forgot to pray. So Verona's older sister, who arrived only a few minutes ago, has suggested that we now have a few moments of prayer."

There is a roar of disapproval. Someone calls out that she is not against Christianity, but it is Saturday night after all! "We will go to church and ask for forgiveness tomorrow!"

Margaret begs for respect for those who prefer to worship God all the time, and after a little while all the guests have calmed down and are sitting quietly.

Verona's sister takes the microphone. "Ladies, my name is Mrs Madombwe, and I am the wife of the Reverend Madombwe of the Children of God Church. Allow me a brief word of prayer, and then I will disappear and leave you to your celebrations." She pauses and looks around. No-one moves. "Let us pray," begins Mrs Madombwe. Her accent has changed into deep American. "Lord, we thank you for the gift of childbirth. It is you who creates life and takes it. Bless the life in Verona's womb."

"Amen!" a voice calls out.

"Bless these women who are gathered here to be merry. And forgive them, Father, for sometimes they celebrate your gift of life in undesirable ways."

"Amen! Hallelujah, Yahweh the Great!" jeers Rita, making a Black Power salute with her fist. Some of the women are finding it hard to stop giggling.

"Dear Lord Jesus, forgive them for they know not what they do."

"Amen, sister! Praise Jesus!" shouts another woman, imitating an American accent.

"Dear Lord, bless this day. Amen." Mrs Madombwe ends her prayer rather abruptly.

"Oh, when the saints, go marching in . . ." Rita starts singing at the top of her voice, and gradually everyone joins in. Anyone would think that a church service was in progress. When the first song finishes, someone breaks into a Shona song which seems to send the women into a religious ecstasy. Fearing that the religious aspect is taking over, the DJ hurriedly begins to play a Zairean tune and with perfect ease the women switch to sexy *kwasa-kwasa* rhythms. Mrs Madombwe discreetly leaves the party.

"Tomorrow morning, without fail, most of us will be wearing our Christian mothers' uniforms and attending churches," remarks Agnes. "But that does not mean that we cannot have a good time tonight."

"That is true, my sisters. We are all hypocrites!" shouts the very drunken Rita. "From the chief reverend or priest, to the Mother Superior, to Father What's-His-Name and the Virgin herself. We are hypocrites! Who can dispute that!"

Margaret leads Rita away and the party continues. Around ten o'clock, Verona, who has washed all the paint off her face, starts putting her presents into the boot and onto the back seat of her car. It does not seem to matter to the dancing, drunken crowd that the guest of honour is leaving. I see the mid-wife make a quick, reassuring examination of Verona's stomach before hugging her and helping her into the car.

"How sweet!" says Kim. "If people always celebrated motherhood this way, I would definitely have a baby."

"Time to go, mate," I say, dragging her away from yet another 'male' partner.

▰▰▰

I see Kim again the following Saturday. Like Adam and me, she has been invited to the Australian High Commissioner's residence for a cocktail party, which is being held in honour of a team of Australian and Zimbabwean rugby players. There are diplomats from New Zealand, Britain, Angola, Namibia and South Africa among the guests, as well as various Australian expatriates from the corporate sector and some Zimbabwean government officials, most of them from the Department of Foreign Affairs. It is a very formal, restrained atmosphere. I find myself wondering when the alcohol will start loosening up a few of these uptight diplomats.

The residence, a beautiful colonial mansion, is set in eight acres of lovely garden. I see many tall native trees as well as eucalypts, flame trees and bougainvillea. The two-storey white building has imposing pillars at the front entrance; at the back, it overlooks an exquisite, well-watered lawn and a glittering swimming pool. Down past the pool are little rocks arranged like a fortress with a miniature waterfall in their midst. There are grass-thatched changing rooms and, behind them, an all-weather tennis court. This house must have belonged to someone quite rich and powerful in the old colonial days.

There are only three black women here – myself, the wife of one of the Zimbabwean government officials and an elderly waitress. I am wearing a green-and-gold West African robe and an embroidered headscarf. I prefer this kind of traditional clothing because it means that I do not have to compete with the rich diplomats in their expensive designer outfits. With Mozart playing in the background and the three African waiters in their starched white uniforms moving from one group to the other, I could be watching a scene from the colonial past. But I do not really feel out of place here, having had quite a lot of experience of situations where mine has been one of the few black faces among many white ones. The inferiority I used to feel around missionaries when I was a teenager has disappeared with time. And when I arrived, the High Commissioner himself kissed me on the cheek. Why should I feel out of place? After all, this is my country and I am among friends. This is quite different from being the only black person at a party in London, Sydney or Melbourne, I tell myself.

After a few glasses of wine, I leave Adam's side. I do not want people to identify me as a 'wife' and wine certainly makes me feel more confident. A Zimbabwean guy from Foreign Affairs joins me. For a while we speak in English; he thinks I am a diplomat from some other African country and is surprised when I switch to Shona. But our conversation does not last long.

"I don't think we have met. I am Simon Cahill and this is my wife, Wendy." The accent tells me that they are Australians.

"Sikia, nice to meet you." I am used to people mispronouncing my name, so I do not attempt to correct her. Instead, I shake their hands.

Simon and Wendy are visiting Zimbabwe for the first time. They left Melbourne a month ago and have been travelling in England. Tomorrow they are off to Victoria Falls, where they will spend three days, before heading to Lake Kariba. They also intend to visit the Great Zimbabwe ruins, near Masvingo, as well as the Eastern Highlands.

"This is our first visit to Africa and we are looking forward to seeing your beautiful country," says Wendy. "But we have to rush home soon because our daughter is expecting a baby. We have to be back before she drops the bundle." She laughs and adds, "From what we have seen, this is an absolutely beautiful country. Such lovely people, such friendly faces. And one thing I have noticed about you Africans is your clean white teeth. Just look at *your* teeth, Sikia – so white and perfect! How do you people do it?"

I excuse myself and walk away. An elderly waiter offers me some tasty marinated chicken on skewers. I have seen this lovely old man several times, as he has been working here for years.

"Oh, my grandchild. How is your family?" He speaks in Shona to me. It is a relief to slip into my own culture for a few moments.

"Very well, Sekuru. How are you?"

"We are still working, as you can see. It is always good to see you. Can I get you another drink?"

"No thank you, Sekuru." He smiles and moves on, tray in hand. He reminds me so much of my father, except for his humility. I cannot imagine Baba ever being humble towards anyone.

"Sekai, meet Jodie and Sue." Kim introduces me to two British women and leaves me to talk to them. Jodie tells me she arrived in Harare last week; she is here to do a doctoral thesis on women who were combatants in the liberation war. Sue has been here for three months and is working on a paper on African feminism. Jodie wears an African headscarf and Sue has on a colourful handwoven dress. They both hold strong views on the oppression of African women; they also mention that eating meat is a crime. I have met many women like Jodie and Sue.

"I simply do not know where to start," says Jodie. "Do you know any women liberation fighters?"

"A few."

"Oh, really? Could you introduce me to them?"

"I could. But what exactly are you trying to research?" I am trying hard not to sound sceptical about Western feminist research.

"Well, I would like to know about the role the women played in the war, what they are doing now and what the future is going to be like for them."

"It is now sixteen years since the war ended." I suddenly feel a little defensive.

"I know. That's why I am interested in knowing what the government has done for these women. Did they get the benefits that men got? Are they being treated equally?"

I am ambivalent about Jodie and Sue's research. Three years ago I attended an academic conference in Melbourne at which I presented a poorly researched paper called 'Who Should Speak for Whom? African Women and Western Feminism'. In it, I argued that Western women should not speak about African women's issues because women's problems were not the same the world over; by taking the platform away from African women, white women were silencing us, I said.

Since then, I have developed my argument a bit further and now feel that once the power relations between black and white women have been acknowledged, a dialogue on specific issues can begin. But I still cannot help wondering why these middle-class, public-school-educated young women from London choose to study African women.

I think of the female ex-combatants I know. Runako, for instance, who left school to join the freedom fighters in 1975 and returned home at independence. You can see shrapnel scars all over her arms and legs. A warm, pretty mother of four, Runako is now the second wife of a headmaster; she deliberately chose to be a second wife when her first marriage collapsed. She rarely talks about the war. If you ask her whether she got what she wanted after independence she says, "What more can a woman expect? I have a good job as a secretary, and my children's fees are paid by the government. I am able to support my widowed mother and my extended family. What more could independence have offered me?"

Then there is Chipo, who rose to the rank of commander in the war. After independence she went to the Soviet Union and graduated as a biochemist. When she returned to Zimbabwe, her role in the war helped her to win a seat in parliament.

"You are one of the most successful woman ex-combatants. I admire your ability to stand your ground against all those men in parliament," I told Chipo, when I met her at an International Women's Day function.

"It is not that easy," she replied. "But one has to continue the struggle."

"You are a very strong feminist. I admire your guts," said a woman from the American Embassy.

"No, no. Please do not call me a feminist," said Chipo. "I am just an African woman who fights for what I believe to be right."

"Why do you not want to be called a feminist?" the American asked.

"Because I hate labels."

The woman from the American Embassy clearly could not understand Chipo's rejection of the term 'feminist'. But I suspected that the problem lay in how Chipo defined the word. When the American women had left, I asked Chipo what she thought feminism stood for.

"I believe in having a husband and in having children. Feminists do not believe in these things. I do not have children nor do I have a husband, and I see this as a failure. If I was Mrs So-and-So or Mai-someone, the men in parliament would respect me more. Some male MPs have called me a feminist, which to them is the same as calling me a separatist lesbian. I hate that."

I tell Jodie and Sue about Chipo. "Do you know any African women who feel comfortable about calling themselves feminists?" Sue asks.

"No. Not really."

"What about yourself?" Sue is very direct.

"It depends on where I am."

"What do you mean?"

"In 1984 I marched at Greenham Common alongside hundreds of English women. I called myself a feminist then. In 1990 I went out on a Reclaim the Night march with Australian women in Melbourne. Again, I called myself a feminist. I supported and still support a number of issues that Western feminists stand for. But there are many issues where our views differ."

"Such as?"

"Such as the issue of racial difference. I do not believe feminism transcends race."

"But surely you do not have to worry about being black any more?" says Sue. "This country successfully fought against exploitation based on race. Why should racial issues be a problem for you now?"

Our discussion is interrupted by the arrival of the rugby players.

"Broad shoulders, thick necks and sexy bodies," Sue says, admiring the boys as they self-consciously walk past us in their uniforms.

"They're too young," says Jodie.

"Not too young to know about life."

"But if you went out with one of them, what would you talk about? Rugby, rugby and more rugby. Those guys would bore you to death."

"Let me find out for myself," replies Sue, and walks away towards the players.

"Do you know where I can have my hair done in braids?" Jodie asks. Her silky blonde hair shines in the dim light.

"But why do you want to have it plaited? It would cost you a lot of money. Moreover, your hair is naturally thin and slippery – the plaits would not last long."

"I don't care. I am sick of the way I look. I wish I had more interesting hair."

We are never happy with the way we look, I think. Some African women spend hours and hours at the hairdresser getting their hair permed or straightened with chemicals so that they can conform to Western images; others buy long artificial hair extensions and weave-ons, just to be different. Feminists and non-feminists alike, we all want to be different.

"Hi! This is a great house, isn't it?" says a woman I know, coming up to join us. Cheryl is an Australian who has lived here for twenty-five years. She came to Rhodesia on holiday, met a farmer's son and married him within six weeks. They divorced during the war and her ex-husband subsequently moved to South Africa, leaving Cheryl with three children to look after. For the past ten years, she has worked in the marketing section of an Australian company.

"Look at those guys – aren't they gorgeous?" Cheryl laughs croakily and lights a cigarette. "I used to have a boyfriend who was a rugby player. God, was the bastard sexy!"

"I don't find them sexy at all," says Jodie.

"Don't you?" Cheryl blinks smoke out of her eyes. "If only I was young again – I could easily take one home tonight."

"I bet he wouldn't be much fun," says Jodie. "Anyway, in a country full of good-looking men, why would you choose one of those naive rugby boys?"

"Good-looking men? Show me. Where are they?"

Jodie tilts her chin in the direction of several of the men standing around, black as well as white.

"You're not talking about black men as well, are you?" asks Cheryl.

"Of course. In fact, I was *only* pointing to black men," says Jodie.

"Here we go. Not the black man fantasy thing again! Give us a break, will you?"

"Why not? I find some of these guys just so sexy."

"So you believe in the fantasy, do you? Maybe we should ask Sekai. Being married to a white man, she is in a position to make comparisons. What do you think, Sekai? Are black men better at it?"

This is not the first time I have been asked that question. Over the years, I have developed a standard answer. "It really makes no difference. All men are created the same way."

"But they differ in performance," says Jodie. "I had a Nigerian boyfriend once. Then I had a Ghanaian one. Both of them were fantastic – in bed and out of it."

"I have lived in this country for twenty-five years and never, in all that time, have I been tempted to go out with a black man," says Cheryl firmly.

"But what is the difference? Why wouldn't you go out with a black man?" asked Jodie.

"The idea is just repulsive to me. But don't get me wrong – I am not a racist or anything like that."

There are two types of white people in Zimbabwe – white Zimbabweans and Rhodies. White Zimbabweans are liberal in their attitudes to race, support the government and work towards the general wellbeing of Zimbabwean society. Rhodies are the die-hards, the rednecks who still wish they were in Rhodesia. Although Rhodies often argue that they are not racists, they remain convinced that they are superior to black people. The more Cheryl talks, the more wine she drinks, the more she reveals a Rhodie side that has not been apparent at our two previous meetings.

"Now tell us honestly, Sekai, how do people treat you in Australia?" she asks me.

"What do you mean?" I ask, already on the defensive.

"I mean, what do people say when they see that you are married to a white man? Being as dark as you are, surely when you go out with Adam and the children, people must find you a strange family. Tell us, how often has someone said that they find it odd to see you together?"

"Not once. Of course people do look at us, but they do not stop and stare. In fact, people smile at the children. I am not saying that Australians are not racists – in many ways they are, but they are subtle about it."

"I'm surprised," says Cheryl as if she does not quite believe me.

"You have such hang-ups about race," said Jodie. "What does it matter what colour a person is?"

"No, it's not a hang-up," says Cheryl. "I just find mixed marriages a bit strange. In fact, I think the whole idea is wrong. I have absolutely nothing against you as a person, Sekai. Believe me, I like you. But I do think that inter-racial marriages should not take place."

I am beginning to feel hot under the collar and a number of insults are forming in my mind. Should I tell this woman exactly what I think of her? But this is a very 'civilised' atmosphere and it would be silly of me to start an argument. So I simply excuse myself and walk away.

"Don't pay any attention to what Cheryl says." Jodie has followed me. Kim sees us together and comes over. Jodie does not hesitate to tell her about Cheryl's views on mixed marriages. Kim puts her arms around my shoulders and says, "You have our apologies. Cheryl ought to do us all a great favour and keep her ideas to herself. I'll make sure she apologises to you."

It is very kind of her to try and fight my war, but I do not want her pity. I am so angry. And the irony is that I felt so comfortable and relaxed when I arrived! It is rather sad to realise that Mugabe's reconciliation policy has made such little impact on Rhodie thinking. Wishing I were back in the village, I leave my white friends and go looking for a drink. The elderly waiter I spoke to earlier comes up to offer me more wine.

"How is your evening progressing, my grandchild?"

I tell him about Cheryl.

"Oh, grandchild, do not take it to heart," says the old man. "Here at the residence I serve many Rhodies and many people who still call me 'boy', but I do not complain because I know who I am. Calling me 'boy' does not take anything away from me. Go on, have more wine to drink, and forget about this ignorant woman. You must realise that sixteen years of independence is not long enough to change some people's attitudes."

I know that he is right. I ought to have known that without being told, just as I know that some black people are every bit as racist as the Rhodies.

The old waiter moves gracefully away with his tray. I watch him go straight up to Cheryl. Putting on a wide smile, he bows his head and offers her another drink.

CHAPTER 10

A Walk with Amai

IT WAS AN unusually cold July morning. The sun rose in a huge yellow arc over the hills. As my mother and I walked down to the valley, I watched it grow smaller. When I was a child, there were winter mornings when Amai used to wake me up early to do an errand and I hated the cold then. But today, I knew she was doing one of her 'business before sunrise' jobs and I volunteered to come along with her.

My mother had several steers but only a couple of cows and one heifer, so she wanted to find a family who would exchange a heifer for an old steer; or, failing that, someone who would simply sell a heifer without entering into an exchange.

"It is not good to have too many steers in the kraal," said Amai. "Apart from pulling the plough, they are not very productive." She knew that people did not voluntarily offer to exchange heifers for steers. "But if you talk to them nicely in the privacy of their homes, they will often gladly give away a beautiful heifer and accept a steer. Or they may sell you an animal if they need quick cash."

Heifers had played an important part in my family's history. "If it were not for my skill at raising good heifers, which became good cows and bred many calves, I would not have been able to send all of you to school after your father died," my mother often said. Each year, when we were growing up, she sold a steer and bought a new heifer. With the little profit she made, she paid for our school fees, books and uniforms.

Once, on Boxing Day, Charity, Constance and I thought we would sleep in and enjoy the holiday. But Amai had other ideas. At the first cock's crow, she woke us up: "Quick, get up. I want you to go down to Weston's place and bring back a new heifer I bought from him. I have heard rumours that it could be pregnant. So go and get it before he changes his mind."

Reluctantly, we got dressed and walked in the moonlight through the mountains to Weston's village. After what seemed to be hours, we realised that dawn had still not broken. Then we heard another cock crow, and Charity said, "Amai has made a mistake. She woke us up well before dawn. It must be four o'clock in the morning." So we decided to cuddle each other and sleep under a tree until sunrise. A disgruntled hyena walked past us as we settled down. Charity yelled loudly at it and it fled. "Hyenas do not attack people," said Charity. "They only squirt shit on you and run away." Constance and I did not believe her until we actually saw the warm excrement near us.

At sunrise we walked down to the Save valley, where Weston lived. Although he did not really want to part with the heifer, Weston had to sell it because his only son was in high school and he needed money for the boy's school fees.

It took us children all morning and afternoon to get the heifer back home, trying to force it to come with us by pulling it along on a leash. That grey heifer, which we named Boxing, gave us five new cows and countless buckets of milk.

"If you want something, think seriously about it and then rise up before dawn and do it," was always Amai's advice. "Never ever let the sun rise before you do. One day, when you get married, your in-laws will think you are lazy if you do not rise at dawn."

In those days I believed that I would get married in a village and become a faithful, hard-working daughter-in-law. I still have a habit of getting up early even if all I want to do is to make a cup of coffee. My sisters are the same. Charity, who lives in New York, says she feels guilty if the early-morning rays come in through her window while she is still in bed. "I simply have to get up, even if I do not have much to do," she says. "Fortunately during a New York winter you hardly see the sun."

And so this morning Amai and I were up early again. Amai walked quickly in front of me, wearing her Australian-made bedroom slippers, an old pair of thick men's socks and a wrap-around cloth to keep her dress from getting dirty. The morning was to be devoted not only to the search for heifers but to visiting our neighbours and catching up on the village gossip as well.

"When you were a baby, I carried you down to the valley, past Weston's place, crossed the Save River and walked all the way to a village beyond those mountains," my mother said, pointing to the distant blue range. "Just over the mountains is a very long road that winds through dark forests where you do not hear the voice of a single soul," said Amai. "The only sounds are those of a dove calling out to her lover or the monkeys breaking twigs as they spy on you. The mountains are haunted. They scare even me after so many years. But I crossed them one day – by myself."

Looking at the hazy mountains across the valley, I asked, "But what were you doing over there? Were you looking for a heifer?"

This was the first time I had heard that Amai had ever crossed the Save River. The river was scary – full of ferocious crocodiles and hippos; there were very few places where you could cross it without danger. But the Save flowed through a fertile valley. Farmers like Weston lost many goats and calves to the crocodiles but this did not deter them from farming along the river.

I remembered the sad story of a niece of Weston's who went to fetch some water at the wrong waterhole when she was visiting her uncle. A crocodile grabbed her arm and, although she struggled and got away, her hand was so badly mauled that it had to be amputated in Wedza. Village people living along the banks of the Save would tell you that Weston's niece ought to have introduced herself to the river and the crocodiles before daring to fetch water. Many sacred spirits lived in the Save River. Late at night, the villagers said, they would hear songs and drums as traditional ceremonies were performed by spirit people who lived hidden in dark, deep waterholes.

"Do water spirits still take people away to train them as traditional healers?" I asked Amai.

"Did they ever do that?"

"Well, when we were growing up there were always these stories in which we were advised to stay away from deep waterholes if we did not want water sprits to capture us. Because if they did, no-one saw or heard about you for many years, but your people would know that the water spirits were keeping you safe and training you to be a traditional healer. After many years, you were released and people welcomed you back to the village with massive celebrations. From then on, you were a *n'anga*."

"I think that may have happened long ago – before our great-grandparents were born," said Amai. Trying to speak to her about myths and folktales never yielded much: she was always sceptical. So I returned to my original question.

"Why did you cross the Save River by yourself?" I imagined

myself as a baby on the back of this little woman. She must have been quite strong, more than thirty years ago.

"Mai Keti had run away from her husband, Chimusoro. She met a man, a salt trader from behind those mountains on the other side of the river. They fell in love and she took her four-year-old child with her and ran away one night. Her lover helped her to carry the child. Mai Keti was a wild horse. Chimusoro was her third husband."

"So how were you involved?"

"Mai Keti and Mai Hilda were my best friends. When you were born, those two helped me deliver you. In those days if anyone came to visit me and I was not home, all they had to do was ask Mai Keti or Mai Hilda where I was. Likewise, if anyone was looking for one of them and couldn't find them, they would ask me where my friend was. That was the reason why Chimusoro came straight to me when Mai Keti disappeared. There was a rumour going round the villages that she had run away with the salt trader and that I was the only one who knew where she had gone."

"And did you know?"

"I knew that Mai Keti had fallen in love with this stranger called Gwede from a village somewhere near Wedza. In fact, she had met him at my place. For many nights she came to sit in my kitchen while he talked about his village and his people."

"But what did Chimusoro say when she was seeing this man so often at night? Surely he must have noticed that his wife was up to something."

"Chimusoro had two other wives and he always came home late. Anyway, it really did not matter whether Mai Keti was there or not. By the time Mai Keti came to live at Chimusoro's place, it was a known fact that he was blind."

"Blind? I did not know he was blind."

Amai laughed. "I do not mean blind in the sense of his eyes not seeing. He developed an enlarged prostate and he could no longer perform according to his wife's expectations. We just say a man is blind when that happens. Of course, not many men admit to it."

"So Mai Keti ran away with Gwede because Chimusoro was 'blind'?"

"That was the reason she gave. But I think she just wanted an adventure. Remember, Chimusoro was her third husband and he was not Keti's father. So anyway, Chimusoro knocked on my bedroom door one morning and demanded that I bring his wife back."

"But it was not your fault that she had run away!"

"I know. But Chimusoro held me responsible all the same. He said that I had planned the escape and that if I wanted to live in the village, I had to bring Mai Keti back. You see, Chimusoro was the headman at the time, so I had to listen to him. I asked your grandparents to take care of my home while I went in search of her. They were genuinely worried about me because none of our people ever crossed the Save and we knew that Gwede's village was on the other side. Mai Hilda offered to come with me but I did not want to put her life in danger as well. What if she was eaten by a crocodile or bitten by a snake? I preferred to make the journey alone."

"And did you find the village?" I asked, as we were crossing a small creek.

"Yes, I did. But when I finally got there, I was on the verge of starvation. You see, I had set out thinking that I would find the village soon after crossing the Save – but in fact it was miles and miles away, and I had had nothing to eat all that time. And although I was warmly welcomed by Mai Keti when I finally arrived, I was given nothing to eat because Gwede was such a poor man that all they could offer me was a huge mug of beer. I was so thirsty and hungry that I could not say I did not drink alcohol. And how would I generate breast milk to feed you if I did not drink the beer? So the day I found Mai Keti was the day I started drinking alcohol!"

"Was it difficult to persuade her to return with you?"

"Not really. Once I had a chance to talk to her alone, I told her I would not go back without her. I told her what Chimusoro had said and she immediately understood that if I returned without her I would be ostracised by everyone in the village. She was my friend and she did not want that to happen. So she spent one more romantic night with Gwede and then we went back to the village together the next day. I was very glad to have her company on the way back – it was much better than walking through the forest on my own, carrying you."

Thinking about my tired, hungry mother walking in the deep forest by herself made me shiver. "You must have been so scared!" I said.

"I was not so much afraid of the forest and the river as of the *mabhinya*."

My heart pounded a little. *Mabhinya* were men who lay in wait in the bush for passers-by whom they would kill in order to use the bodies for witchcraft. There was a belief that if a person greatly desired wealth – to succeed as a businessman for instance – and consulted a witchdoctor on how to achieve his goal, the *n'anga* would tell him to kill someone, take a specific organ – liver, heart, brain or genitals – and follow a set of instructions. If the person wanted to have a successful supermarket, he might be advised to hide the heart of a beautiful girl somewhere in the shop or under the foundation of the building; the spirit of the girl would attract customers to the shop. A person who intended to own a grinding mill might be advised to bury some brains near the mill, and so on.

Although these beliefs were hard to credit, there was no doubt that some people who desperately wanted to get rich quickly would believe whatever a *n'anga* told them. Just last year, there were stories of schoolchildren in Harare disappearing on their way home because they had been kidnapped for witchcraft. One day, when I was waiting in the street for an emergency taxi, a policewoman who saw me advised me never to get into a car without checking whether it was a genuine emergency taxi. I asked her whether there was any truth in the stories about people being murdered for their organs. She replied that this evil practice had always existed, but that it was on the rise because of increasing materialism in society.

"But surely *mabhinya* would not kill a woman carrying a child?" I asked Amai.

"You would be surprised," replied Amai. "Sometimes men get possessed by wild spirits and lose their humanity. Then they can kill, rape or commit other abominable crimes – especially if they are following what a *n'anga* tells them to do. Did not Mandinde sleep with his daughter for many years because he believed that committing incest would make him rich, as a *n'anga* had told him?"

"I remember hearing that years ago. His daughter never married, did she?"

"No. She never married because people knew that Mandinde used her for his own purposes. Now she is a shebeen queen somewhere in Bulawayo. Apparently, she cannot let a man come close to her. Every time one attempts to do so, she remembers her father and physically assaults the man."

"Mandinde was rich, wasn't he? Maybe if you believe in something, it works," I remarked. "I remember his orchard was the biggest around here and his cattle would fill the whole schoolyard. And he was the only one with a grinding mill in the village – people used to wait all day to get their maize ground there. That kind of wealth was unheard of in those days."

"True," said Amai, "but he was doing something evil and everyone knew that one day he was going to pay for it. Sure enough, when the war started, Mandinde was taken away by the comrades one night and was never seen again."

"But there is a grave with his name on it next to the place where his grinding mill used to stand."

"That only came about after the war, when Mandinde's relatives had exhausted all hope of finding his body. We will never know who killed him, where he died or where his body found a resting place."

"But the grave . . . ?" I asked.

"There is a goat's head in that grave," said Amai.

We walked on in silence for a while. In Shona culture, if a person dies away from home, their relatives will do nothing about a ceremony for months, even years, until they are convinced that the body will never be brought to its proper resting place. Then a burial ceremony takes place at which everyone mourns the dead person as if their body were there. But when it comes to the actual burial, a goat's head is buried in the grave. Still, it was hard to believe that Mandinde, that ruthless giant of my childhood, could have disappeared so easily into thin air.

"The war was like that," Amai said, as if reading my thoughts. "It swept away big and small people, rich and poor."

We were approaching VaJanet's homestead. My mother

wanted to avoid it because VaJanet had no cattle and could not have provided us with a heifer.

"Silly woman! She spent so many years on the white man's farm and came home old, tired and penniless," remarked Amai.

But a dog barked as we attempted to skirt VaJanet's courtyard. According to village etiquette, you only avoid someone's home if you have an unresolved conflict with them. So we could not escape VaJanet, a big woman with large, pendulous breasts, who emerged from her tiny hut.

"Who is passing by my courtyard so early in the morning?" she asked.

"It is me, David's wife, and my daughter. We just wanted to ask about your health. We will not go into the house," said Amai.

"Please do come into my humble house. The grandchildren are still asleep but do come in," VaJanet begged us.

Amai politely refused. "We must move on. Last night my two donkeys did not come home and I fear that the hyena might have got hold of them. We will definitely stop by on our way back." This was unlikely to happen, but my mother had to say something to show that she was willing to sit down and chat with VaJanet.

A little further on, we came to another small homestead and managed to sneak past two little huts without being seen. "That is where VaJanet's son and his Malawian wife have recently settled," said Amai. "They do not have anything either, apart from a couple of goats and two chickens. But the Malawian wife is starting to do big business out of teaching women around here how to make Malawi gin. That stuff is strong and as clear as water – I would not touch it!"

We had reached another small creek, and my mother washed her face in the cold water. She wiped her face with a piece of her wraparound cloth and then jumped over the creek. I did the same.

Just then, we saw three women coming towards us. On their heads they carried clay pots which they would fill at the creek.

"Mai Sydney! What brings you this far so early in the morning?" the oldest woman asked.

"My donkeys are missing . . . Err . . . Also, I was wondering whether I could talk to you for a moment?"

"So you were coming to my place?"

I recognised VaMakambaya from her deep voice and the several tattoos on her face. Everyone in the village called her 'the mother of many sons'. Her nine boys were well known for being the best fighters for miles around.

Amai spread her wraparound cloth on the ground and sat on it. VaMakambaya did the same, then took out a small tin that had once contained shoe polish and poured some snuff into the palm of her hand. She offered it to my mother, who took a little pinch, pushed the snuff into her nose and sneezed. I sat down near them, on the banks of the creek.

The two other women, VaMakambaya's daughters-in-law, filled up the clay pots. One of them washed out a couple of nappies, while the other crouched ankle-deep in the creek and let the water splash around her genitals. She talked and laughed, completely at ease, taking no notice of the fact that I was watching her.

It seemed that these women had never been taught about environmental hygiene. Here they were washing nappies and bathing in the same place from which they fetched their drinking water. I watched as the other woman wrung out her two nappies, put them in a plastic bag and then crouched down to let the cold water splash her genitals. I remembered how village women would never cross a stream without taking the opportunity to bathe their private parts. With the heat of the sun and their long hours of hard work, it was difficult to avoid strong body odour, so the women took every chance to wash themselves. And once or twice a week, they would meet down by the water with their laundry. This was a social occasion: the women would swim, bathe, massage each other and catch up with the village gossip.

VaMakambaya's daughters-in-law must have been busy, as they did not sit around by the creek for long. They picked up their water pots, balanced them carefully on their heads and waved to VaMakambaya, who was talking in low tones with Amai.

When the two younger women were out of earshot, VaMakambaya said, "You see that one, the tall one in front? She has started taking pills in order to stop herself from having more children."

"She is Lancelot's wife?"

"Yes, the one who came back to live in the village recently after Lancelot was retrenched from the clothing factory where he had worked for more than twenty years."

"How many children does she have?" asked Amai.

"Only three – one boy and two girls."

"She should have at least two or three more," said Amai. "Small families are the luxury of urban women who think they are white!"

My mother had encouraged Sydney to have six children although she knew very well that he could not really afford to care for them on his teacher's salary. For years, she had tried hard to encourage me and my sisters to have large families too, but without success. What she did not know was that Zimbabwe had one of the lowest birth rates in Africa; in the cities, couples had an average of two children. But among rural families the story was different.

In the villages there was a widespread belief, especially among men, that a woman ought to continue having children until she was too old to do so. Through the services of village health workers, the government had made contraceptives accessible to women, but pressure from their in-laws often forced women to keep having children. A health worker I had recently met had told me that she got a lot of resistance to contraception from Catholics as well as from followers of the Apostolic Faith, who argued that children were a gift from God.

Meanwhile, VaMakambaya was still complaining to my mother. "You know, Lancelot will not allow his wife to take family planning pills. So she tells him that she does not take anything and expects him to believe that his seed just happens to be going to waste."

"But how do you know that your daughter-in-law is taking these pills?" Amai asked.

"Because I found them hidden in the jar of maize meal. These young women hide family planning pills in places where their husbands will never dream of searching. Why would Lancelot put his fingers in a jar of maize meal? Sometimes they hide the pills inside a child's nappy because everyone knows a man would never touch a nappy."

"So did you tell Lancelot that his wife is taking family planning pills?"

"Why should I tell him? It is all up to him. If he decides that his wife is infertile, he will get another wife. And if that happens, those tablets will be thrown in the rubbish bin and within a few months that daughter-in-law of mine will be proudly displaying her pregnancy. Women love competition. Wait and see!" VaMakambaya stood up and folded her cloth. "Mai Sydney, go and see Philemon's wife. I know that she will sell anything to buy herself a sewing machine. Go now. But do not mention that I suggested you speak to her – she likes to keep everything secret."

We left VaMakambaya filling up her water pot and set off for the homestead she had directed us to. I recognised Emilia, Philemon's wife, as soon as we walked into her courtyard. When I was in primary school, she was one of the older ex-students who came back to the school to play football or netball on Friday afternoons. When the home defenders, as they were called, were not playing sport themselves, they acted as cheer leaders when we competed against neighbouring schools.

In those days, primary school went up to Grade Five. Since schooling was free for whites but not for blacks, one black child out of a class of thirty would be lucky to go on to senior school. Emilia, who was in the same primary school class as my sister Constance, was a highly intelligent girl who came first in every subject. Like Constance, Emilia could have been a teacher or a nurse if she had stayed at school. But after she finished Grade Five, her parents could no longer afford to pay her fees and she had to leave school.

At seventeen, Emilia married another home defender, Philemon. Philemon found a job as a porter at the hospital in Marondera and Emilia stayed home in the village. Five years later, the couple had still not produced a child. Although it was equally possible that Philemon could have been infertile, the blame for not having a baby was placed on Emilia.

According to my mother, Emilia's aunt came to visit her niece one day and said, "Emilia, if you do not do something, Philemon will get another wife."

"I know, VaTete. But what can I do?" Emilia was in tears.

"If you are infertile, this is nothing new. We will just have to

191

approach Philemon's family and admit your disability. They will then say that they did not pay five heads of cattle for a woman who cannot renew their birth line, and we will be forced to offer them your sister Ruvimbo. She will become Philemon's second wife. Her children will be your children and in this way the shame of infertility will be removed from you."

"But I have not been proved infertile as yet. Why should Ruvimbo take my husband before I am given a chance to prove myself, VaTete? What if it is Philemon who is infertile?" Emilia asked.

"That is what I was going to ask you, my child. Now, tell me, what is his performance like? Are you confident that his seed is strong enough to produce children? Surely after five years you must know whether he is a strong or a weak man."

"If he was strong, he would have had a child by another woman by now. Every dry season I go and live with him in Marondera, but I have not seen anything to make me suspect that he might be having an affair. VaTete, you know what men are like. If a man thinks that his wife is infertile, he quickly tries his luck with another woman in order to remove the shame of childlessness from himself. If Philemon had tried that and succeeded, then a pregnant woman would have come here to be my co-wife by now. I think my husband could be blind."

VaTete got up from the kitchen bench and checked briefly outside the hut to see that no-one was listening. Then she sat on the floor, lowered her voice and said, "Now, Emilia, listen to me. It is time to allow another man into your bedroom. Look at Philemon's brothers and decide which one you consider to have good seed. Remember, you must first consider one of his brothers or another close member of his family. But if there is no-one suitable, you can then find any lover whose role is to give you children. Do you understand?"

Emilia took a deep breath. "I have thought of that," she said. "As you know, VaTete, Philemon has three brothers – one older than he is and two younger. But they are all married."

"That does not matter, my child. What you want is seed from Philemon's family. You do not need a husband – you have one already."

"I know."

"So, which of the three do you want?" VaTete smiled.

"The older brother suffers from epileptic fits and he does not seem to be intelligent. I do not want to have his children. The second brother is nice, but he is rather short and he never holds down employment for very long. He is also very fair-skinned, to the extent that his nose is covered in freckles. A short, fair child with freckles would give the secret away," Emilia replied.

"That leaves the third brother."

"Yes. Mateo is reasonably tall, clean and quite handsome. In fact, of the three brothers, he is the one who looks most like Philemon. He is also the most educated of them all – he passed his O levels and is training to be a teacher. But the problem is that his wife is quite young and pretty. He will not like the idea of making love to his older sister-in-law." Emilia sounded resigned to failure.

"Leave it to me," said VaTete. "If that is the man whose seed we want, he will do the job. I am certain that his father and grandfather will welcome the idea. They will speak to him and I do not think there will be a problem. This has been our custom for many generations."

During the following school holidays, Mateo and his wife, Chengeto, came to visit Emilia. They had dinner at her house and everything seemed as usual. Emilia thought that Mateo must have declined to participate in the old custom of donating sperm within families. But a few days later, he knocked on Emilia's door just before midnight. Emilia welcomed him and he came back for several nights in a row. Chengeto did not know of these visits and the following week Mateo went back to college. Immediately he'd gone, VaTete told Emilia to hurry to Marondera and spend a month with Philemon. She did so, and nine months later gave birth to a beautiful baby boy who was the spitting image of Philemon.

Although the secret was known by most people in the village by then, if Philemon knew that he was not the child's father, he pretended that he was; this was expected of him. As the years went by, Emilia had four children – one boy and three girls. As for Mateo, he went on living in Harare with Chengeto and their two children.

Emilia greeted Amai and me warmly, ushered us into her smoky little kitchen hut and began preparing tea. Amai mentioned that she wanted to buy a heifer and asked Emilia if, by any chance, she might have one to sell.

"I need money," Emilia replied. "My son is at boarding school and we cannot afford to pay his fees. If not for his uncle Mateo's help, he could not have gone as far as he has done in his schooling. But Mateo has his own responsibilities and we cannot rely on him for too long." She added a whole cup of sugar to the teapot and stirred it in. I did not say that I had stopped taking sugar many years ago; in the villages, tea without sugar is not regarded as tea.

Emilia served us sweet potatoes with the tea. "I will sell my heifer to you, although I would have loved to keep it," she said. "With the money, I will go to South Africa and buy a sewing machine. Then I will be able to make school uniforms and sell them at the local schools."

Emilia was one of many hard-working women whose economic survival depended on buying goods in South Africa or Botswana and reselling them in Zimbabwe. Over the past five years, Emilia had got used to spending a full day waiting in the queue for visa applications at the South African Embassy in Harare. It would take her twelve hours on a crowded bus to get to Johannesburg. Because she could not afford to pay for accommodation, she would have to spend the night sleeping on the floor at the bus station – a scary place that was notorious for rape and robbery.

The following morning, in the company of other women traders from Zimbabwe, she would go to outlets in Johannesburg where consumer goods could be bought cheaply. By late afternoon, she would be back on the bus to Zimbabwe with her purchases. At the Beitbridge border post, Emilia and the other women would be harassed by customs officers and would have to pay duty on their goods. But once they were back home, the women could sell their goods at three times the price they had paid. In this way many Zimbabwean women from the lower socio-economic sector were able to provide a major boost to their families' income.

Most of the women engaged in this business were from the cities; Emilia was one of the few rural women who had succeeded in penetrating the trade. She had done well, even managing to finance the building of a three-bedroom house and the construction of a borehole. But there were so many stories about Zimbabwean women being raped or murdered in South Africa that Philemon decided that he no longer wanted Emilia to travel down south over the border.

"But I asked him to allow me to go just one more time," said

Emilia. "He agreed, so I am going to buy a sewing machine in South Africa and then start sewing school uniforms for a living."

She agreed to sell her heifer for fifteen hundred dollars and my mother paid her a third of the amount as a deposit. "Do not tell anyone about this," begged Emilia. "My in-laws will say that I am selling their son's wealth. They forget that every single cow in that kraal has been bought with my sweat."

"But they will know, sooner or later," Amai said.

"I know. But by then, they will not be able to stop me. Tell Simba, your herd boy, to bring your cattle to our grazing pastures on Friday. I will instruct my herd boy to meet him with our cattle, and then Simba can just quietly take the heifer home with the rest of your cattle."

Emilia accompanied us out into her courtyard. As we were saying goodbye, we saw Philemon's father approaching. Emilia giggled and whispered, "Bad timing today. At least two or three times a week he comes here to have tea and something to eat with us. He has a wife who should cook for him. Why should I feed him so often?"

"But it is the duty of all daughters-in-law to feed their husbands' elderly fathers," said Amai. "As he gets older, Philemon's father will depend a lot more on you and less on his wife. In fact, very soon Philemon's mother will also need looking after."

"I know. But what do I get from it?" Emilia asked. My mother did not reply, because Philemon's father was within earshot.

"Oh, David's wife! What brings the Buffalo this far so early in the morning?" My mother's totem was the buffalo, so she was often called by that name.

"Greetings, Monkey. How is your health? I came this way with my daughter in search of two lost donkeys," Amai lied again. "Have you perhaps seen them this way?"

I realised that village people never wanted it known that they had cash. If Amai had said that she wanted to buy a heifer, someone would have come to her that very day asking to borrow money. Inevitably, their need would be urgent, and Amai would have to forget about the heifer for a while and lend the money. And getting money back was always such a hassle that my mother, like the other village people, preferred not to lend it in the first place.

"No, Buffalo. I do not think your donkeys came our way," the old man said.

"Good morning, father. Did you sleep well?" Emilia gave a little curtsy and clapped her hands.

"Good morning, my daughter. I was just coming to your place for a nice cup of sweet tea. Without you, I cannot survive in this village."

"But you still have your wife," Amai said.

"Yes, but what use is she to me? Apart from providing the usual boring meal of *sadza* and vegetables, she is of no use at all." Then, grinning and revealing several missing teeth, the old man looked at me and added, "If I were to find a healthy young woman like this one, I would pay everything I have. What do you say, young lady, eh?"

We all laughed. "Why would she waste her time on an old man?" Emilia said.

"You never know what an old man can do! You go your way, Buffalo, and I will see you sometime," said Emilia's father-in-law, and disappeared into the kitchen hut.

"I better go back," said Emilia. "Otherwise I will find the old man helping himself to the whole jar of sugar!" She shook hands with us and ran back inside.

Amai told me that Emilia adored her father-in-law, although she resented his frequent visits. "After all, he has kept the secret of Philemon's infertile condition for so long. When Mateo stopped coming back to the village, that old man arranged for one of Philemon's cousins to enter Emilia's bedroom so she could have the last two children."

Walking back home behind Amai, I wondered what would have happened if Adam or I had been unable to have children. I could not imagine Adam's brother Simon secretly entering my bedroom to donate his sperm to me. But wasn't this traditional practice a good solution to the anguish of infertility? Perhaps I could have accepted that form of surrogacy after all, if Adam had been 'blind' . . . But as for my sisters or pretty nieces bearing Adam's children in my place, the mere thought filled me with horror!

CHAPTER 11

A Forgotten People

I N NORTH-WESTERN Zimbabwe lies a remote region known as Omay. Hot, dry and ridden with tsetse flies and mosquitoes, Omay combines barren terrain with thick jungle full of wild animals. Visiting this regions is like going back in time.

The people of Omay belong to an ethnic group known as the Tonga or Batonka. For as far back as they could remember, the Tonga had lived along the valley on either side of the mighty Zambezi River. A semi-nomadic people, they knew nothing of farming. The Zambezi River provided them with several varieties of fish, and wild animals and fruits were plentiful in the river valley, so the Tonga did not go hungry. Further south, the Ndebele and the Shona carried on their violent feuding, but the Tonga remained very much a secluded group, living peacefully except for the occasional fight between families.

But life was to change dramatically for the Tonga. In 1953, the British divided parts of their southern African colonial territories into a federation comprising Northern Rhodesia (Zambia), Nyasaland (Malawi) and Southern Rhodesia (Zimbabwe). No longer could a Tonga simply cross the Zambezi in his canoe to visit a relative; he needed a passport, as the river had become the border between Northern and Southern Rhodesia.

Just when the Tonga were getting used to these formalities, and the gunshots of the border patrols, the colonial government announced that it intended to dam the Zambezi River. Construction began on Kariba Dam, Africa's largest hydroelectric project at the time, and the Tonga were told they would have to leave the river valley. Their traditional lands would be flooded by the new lake, Lake Kariba, which would be 200 kilometres long and up to forty kilometres wide. They would no longer have access to the river.

Black African government officials, accompanied by white men, came to visit the Tonga chiefs and explained that the new lake was necessary because the country needed hydroelectric power. They told the chiefs that their people were to be moved to the Zambezi Escarpment. No-one had ever lived in this wild, dry country – and for good reason.

"How can we survive without the river?" argued the chiefs. "Our fathers and grandfathers lived along the river for many generations. We do not want to be moved."

But it was not long before armed policemen arrived and forced the Tonga people to move away from the river valley. Although the Tonga tried to fight back, they had to accept that their spears were useless against the policemen's guns.

"Stop fighting – a good supply of electricity will benefit your community," urged the government officials. But the Tonga could not care less about electricity; what they needed was water and fish from their river. So they appealed to Nyaminyami, the fish-headed, serpent-tailed god of the Zambezi, for assistance. But Nyaminyami seemed to have forgotten them. By 1955, the chiefs had been forced to settle on higher ground, in the region that became known as Omay.

Many workers, both black and white, were employed in the construction of the dam; many of them lost their lives, as the work was conducted at breakneck speed to fit into the political timetables of the white governments of the federation. The chiefs concluded that Nyaminyami was taking their sons' lives because he was against the construction of the dam. Tearfully, they collected the dead whose bodies could be salvaged and buried them at the new settlements. The colonial government also mourned its dead, burying them at the Church of Saint Barbara in Kariba. By 1958, the main dam wall was complete, the lake began filling and the government celebrated what it called 'the jewel of an inland sea'.

Without access to the river, the Tonga depended largely on hunting for survival. Wild animals were abundant, even in Omay. But then the government introduced the Protection of Wildlife Act, which required hunters to have permits. The Tonga found such bureaucracy bewildering; and in any case, most of them could not afford the fees required to obtain a permit. Fishing in the new lake was subject to similar regulations.

With hunting and fishing restricted, the Tonga began to experience hunger. Meanwhile, tourism was starting to develop at Lake Kariba. The Tonga watched as a five-star hotel went up, followed by a number of holiday resorts and safari camps. Small aeroplanes would land on the runways around the lake and groups of white people wearing safari outfits and carrying binoculars and cameras would emerge to be driven away to their hotels and lodges. In the early evening, the white tourists would cruise slowly past in motorboats, drinking beer or wine while they watched the sunset.

When the war for independence began in the mid-1960s, many young Tonga men, the bitter wounds of their dispossession still fresh in their minds, crossed the border into Zambia to join the training camps of the freedom fighters. Like the Shona and Ndebele, these young people were driven by the desire to reclaim their land. For some years, the struggle raged back and forth across the border; freedom fighters sporadically attacked holiday resorts and for several years tourists no longer came to the lake.

When independence came in 1980 the Tonga celebrated, hoping that their problems were over. The elderly chiefs dreamt of returning to their old homes. But it was not long before they realised that independence would change very little for them. In fact, the new government placed even more restrictions on hunting and fishing. More hotels were built around Lake Kariba and tourists started coming back. The Tonga continued to watch and wait, while several severe droughts brought unprecedented poverty to Omay. "The new government has forgotten us," mourned the chiefs.

The plight of their people did not go unnoticed by Western non-governmental organisations. "We will teach the Tonga how to farm," declared a zealous young aid worker in an air-conditioned office in Melbourne. "We will build schools for them," said his counterpart in Oslo. "They do not have cattle because of the tsetse flies, so let's give them tractors to plough the land," said a New Yorker. A group of English workers from the Save the Children Fund flew to Omay and began to teach the locals how to grow vegetables. UNICEF introduced feeding programmes for all children under five. And a women's church group in Denmark sent the Tonga truckloads of secondhand clothes.

▰▰▰

In July 1996, I went to Omay as one of the 'Western' aid workers committed to sustainable development in the region. An Australian friend of mine had called one morning to ask if I was interested in going to Omay to evaluate an agricultural development project. She briefed me on the region and promised to pay me generously if I could spend a couple of days up there and then write a report on how Australian aid was being used in Omay. In high school I had seen photographs of bare-breasted Tonga women sitting submissively around their warriorlike husbands. Apart from these postcard images, I knew nothing about the Tonga people.

I was to be accompanied on my journey by two Zimbabwean project officers working in Omay. I met the two young men, Thomas and Tapiwa, and we agreed to set off the following day at noon. It was going to be an eight to nine-hour drive, they told me.

As agreed, I was ready for my companions at noon the following day. It all seemed rather ironic. There I was, dressed up like a Westerner – sunhat, sunglasses, brown safari skirt and blouse, and comfortable walking boots. I had even gone as far as spreading sunscreen all over my face and arms. "It is a myth that black people do not burn," I remembered Charity telling me; I had not believed her until I noticed how much darker I became after each visit to the village.

Thomas and Tapiwa did not turn up until half-past three. Thomas, who was at the wheel of a very flash four-wheel drive, was not at all apologetic for the delay. "African time," laughed Tapiwa, as he opened the back door for me.

"We should be at Siakobvu, the central administration office in Omay, by midnight," said Thomas.

The drive from Harare to Kadoma was uneventful, the road

being wide and tarred; black Zimbabweans still often thank the colonial government for putting a very good infrastructure in place between major towns. Soon after Kadoma, we branched off towards Gokwe, formerly a small shopping centre, which had flourished since independence. Once farmed exclusively by whites, Gokwe district was now a resettlement area where African farmers grew cotton. Tsetse flies had been eradicated in the area, new industries were being set up and government offices and houses were being built everywhere.

We pulled into town shortly before seven. Thomas parked in front of a nightclub called the Talk of Gokwe.

"We will eat here today," said Tapiwa, leading me into a large room with a bar and a dusty cement floor. On one side of the room were two or three men drinking beer. Next to them sat two young women sipping Fanta. "Early birds," said Tapiwa, looking at the women. Dressed in jeans, runners and T-shirts, the two aid workers looked smart and affluent in comparison with the locals.

"Welcome, welcome comrades," said the middle-aged man behind the bar. He shook hands with Thomas and Tapiwa, ignoring me. I gathered that he assumed I was Tapiwa or Thomas's girlfriend.

"It is getting late, guys," continued the barman. "I suggest you stay the night here. Driving on these roads after dark is terribly hazardous." But Thomas told him that we had to move on after dinner.

Dinner was served in the nightclub's stuffy restaurant. We sat on plastic chairs at a wooden table covered with a red tablecloth. The menu didn't offer much choice: *sadza* and beef stew, *sadza* and tripe or fried chicken with chips and salad. To my regret, I chose the chicken; the chips arrived soggy, oily and cold, the chicken seemed to have been deep-fried for the tenth time, and the salad consisted of strips of cabbage and carrots in vinegar and a single slice of tomato covered in grey spots. I enviously watched Thomas and Tapiwa eating *sadza* and tripe with their fingers.

"You can never go wrong with *sadza*. Chicken and chips are for Westerners," said Tapiwa, guzzling down his third beer.

Thomas drained his second beer and ordered another. "We work for a religious non-governmental agency," he reminded me, "so do not mention to anyone that we drank beer on this trip. You understand, don't you, that working in the bush would not be much fun without beer – we would be bored to death."

"We will have a few more beers, then we will have just a few more, and then we will be on our way," laughed Tapiwa, getting up. I wondered who was going to drive, given that both of them were drinking.

When we returned to the bar after dinner, it was almost full. Music blared, and there were people of all ages drinking and talking loudly. What was most striking about the crowd was that the women were much younger than most of the men. I managed to find a seat near the wall. Thomas and Tapiwa disappeared in the direction of the bar and did not return, so I decided that I was going to entertain myself by striking up a conversation with the woman sitting next to me.

"I have not seen you here before," said Liza, who must have been in her twenties.

"I am just passing through on my way to Omay," I explained.

"That is what everyone says when they first come to Gokwe!" she laughed. "No-one ever admits that they are looking for business. Let me see if I can guess what happened. You met a nice young man. He promised to marry you, but one day you found that you were pregnant and he was nowhere to be seen.

You needed a job to support yourself and your child, so you came to Gokwe in search of employment as a domestic worker – or as anything respectable. But you could not find a job, so you turned to the oldest profession in the world."

"Who is she?" asked a young girl who came up to Liza with a drink.

"Passing through, she says," said Liza. The two of them laughed.

"Aren't we all passing through?" said the girl sarcastically. She could not have been much older than fifteen. She sat down on the other side of me, introduced herself as Priscilla and began talking to Liza across me, complaining that business was slow.

"It is mid-month – a difficult time," said Liza. "Well, difficult with young men! It is never difficult with the old cotton-growers. They give you up to forty dollars for the night if you are lucky."

"Only forty dollars?" I asked.

The two girls laughed again. "How much do you expect? The price is forty dollars for the night in your house or thirty dollars at his house," said Liza. "Although with the young men, a girl's lucky to get twenty dollars at her house. They are so stingy."

"Worse still, they will try to pay only twenty dollars for sex without a condom," said Priscilla.

Turning to me, Liza began to teach me the rules of the trade in Gokwe. "Never accept twenty dollars for sex without a condom. It is not worth getting AIDS for. If he says sixty dollars without a condom, go for it. But do not accept anything less."

"But is even sixty dollars worth the risk of AIDS?" I asked, incredulously.

"What difference does it make? If you are unlucky you will get AIDS whether you do or do not use a condom. You try to use condoms at first, but men will tell you that they will not eat a sweet that is still inside its wrapper – meaning that sex is not as good if you use a condom. Men have to get their money's worth, you know."

"And even if you get the virus today, it will not show for some years," said Priscilla. "So why deprive yourself and your children while you still have the opportunity to make money and buy nice things?"

A man in his fifties or sixties lurched towards us. "Three beers here?" he asked hopefully.

"Liza's regular sugar daddy," whispered Priscilla. "He is a successful cotton-grower with three wives at home. He pays well."

As Liza went off with the cotton-grower to the bar, Thomas and Tapiwa returned from wherever they had been.

"Sister, let us move on," said Tapiwa.

"Lucky girl!" said Priscilla. "You have got two in one go. Why don't you give me one?"

"They are my brothers," I said, standing up. I shook Priscilla's hand and slipped twenty dollars into her palm. She looked at me in amazement and I followed my 'brothers' out of the Talk of Gokwe.

The night drive from Gokwe to Siakobvu was as dangerous as the barman had warned. Although it was tarred for most of the way, the road wound treacherously as we climbed the Zambezi Escarpment. At least four times we nearly hit donkeys, goats or cows which had wandered onto the road. This was the start of the wild country; if our car had careered off the road, we might not have been found for months. Luckily, despite all the beer he had drunk, Thomas drove very well.

Just after the road gave way to dirt, Tapiwa applied the brakes suddenly and the car screeched to a halt.

"What is the matter?" I asked in panic.

"An elephant is lying on the road. He seems to be asleep," said Tapiwa, peering cautiously through the windscreen into the distance. Sure enough, the headlights showed that on the road up ahead lay a huge elephant, probably one of a herd that was concealed in the trees beside the road.

"You should never get out of your car around here," warned Thomas. "We are in a wildlife area and the animals can be quite hostile if you disturb them." With a bit of persuasion from the car horn, the huge beast finally rose and lumbered away into the forest.

It was well after midnight when we arrived in Siakobvu, where most of the government offices administering the Omay region were located. We were to spend what was left of the night at one of the guesthouses where visitors were accommodated. The project clerk, who had faithfully waited up for us, showed me to a small room. The facilities were very basic; there was no hot water in the bathroom and no sheets on my single bed. As I was falling asleep, I heard the sounds of elephants and lions somewhere in the deep forest that surrounded us. A very high electric fence, constructed with European Union grant money, protected the people and the buildings from the wildlife.

⚊⚊⚊

The following morning Nyati, the project clerk, served us sweet tea, bread and a boiled egg each for breakfast. Thomas had work which would keep him busy at the Siakobvu office for the next few days, but Tapiwa said that he would take me to Chief Msambakaruma's area, where I was to meet the Tonga chief and hear about how his people had benefited from Australian aid money.

So, after breakfast, we set off along a very bad dirt road. Along the way we passed children heading for school. Tapiwa told me that they probably had to walk between ten and fifteen kilometres each way. "As far as education is concerned, this is the most neglected area in Zimbabwe."

We drove for about sixty kilometres before arriving at Chief Msambakaruma's compound. We were greeted by his elderly first wife, who was sitting in the shade of a mango tree surrounded by several young children. She told us that the chief had gone to the nearby shopping centre where he was waiting for us.

"Chief Msambakaruma's father was the last person to be forced to move from the Zambezi valley," Tapiwa told me, as we drove on.

We found the chief sitting on a stool in the shade near the small cluster of shops. A couple of his councillors were sitting on the ground nearby; I was surprised to see that they were not Tonga but Shona. A bronze necklace and a walking stick decorated with threaded black and white beads were the only symbols of Msambakaruma's chiefly status; it would have been easy to mistake this powerful chief for an ordinary man. Tapiwa offered to fetch me a chair but I told him that I preferred to sit on the ground, next to the chief's councillors.

"Welcome, daughter of the soil!" said Chief Msambakaruma. "The world is changing. When these men told me that an Australian woman was coming to visit me, I thought that she would be a white person. It is good to see that our own children can do the jobs that were done by white people before."

The chief then went on to ask for more aid so that he could continue to teach his people how to grow cotton. After two or three beers, provided courtesy of Tapiwa, the chief asked me to go to Australia and tell those white people that he needed electricity and a borehole at his house. I thought of the grand promises the Rhodesian government had made to the Tonga about the electricity and development that would come with the gigantic lake that had flooded their lands.

I promised the chief that I would tell the aid agency of his people's needs. As Tapiwa and I were getting ready to leave, one of the councillors invited us to his house, a short way down the dusty road. We were greeted by his wife, who to my surprise served us fresh curds made from cow's milk.

"I thought that due to the tsetse flies, no-one was allowed to have cattle around here," I said.

"They are permitted in some areas ruled by Chief Msambakaruma," replied the councillor's wife. She went on to tell me that she and her husband had been living in Omay for five years. They were originally from Masvingo, but the land they had owned there was difficult to farm. "A cousin of ours in Gokwe knew Chief Msambakaruma, so we came here to ask him for land. For only two hundred dollars we got huge plots of virgin land which we cleared. Now we grow cotton, groundnuts and maize. Although most of Omay is dry and infertile, some parts are good to farm. And unlike the Tonga people, we are not lazy."

Our next destination was an irrigation project funded by the Australian government. We had lunch along the way: a bottle of Fanta and two dry buns each. As we ate, I mentioned my surprise at finding Shona migrants in Omay.

"The government is totally against the idea," said Tapiwa. "But the local chiefs still believe that they have the power to allocate land, and do so. Officially, it is the head of the district council who has the authority to decide what happens to the land and the wildlife, and he has to follow government rules that protect the environment. But he must be able to get on with the chiefs, or else they can protest to the government that they do not want him or his council officers around here. The chiefs sell land illegally to migrants, and they encourage slash-and-burn farming so that their people can learn to farm, which they need to do in order to survive. The chiefs also participate in setting traps for wildlife, which is against the law, arguing that the animals are their heritage. How can the council enforce the government regulations? Quite often, the officers turn a blind eye to the chiefs' operations."

We had left Chief Msambakaruma's area and were driving through Chief Mola's lands. I was struck by the clusters of grass-thatched huts we passed. Each village had about twenty to thirty of these little, low-roofed structures, which were quite different from any other traditional architecture I had seen in Zimbabwe.

"In the old days, the Tonga, unlike the Shona and Ndebele, preferred these temporary dwellings," explained Tapiwa. "They would move on to another place after one or two seasons, looking for new fishing grounds. Even today you hardly find a solid house built to last in their villages."

We descended into a valley, the road running down between two mountains. On either side of the road was thick, impenetrable forest. Once or twice we came across a small clearing where a young couple would be busy slashing and burning the bush, preparing the land for crops before the rains came.

"Those girls are likely to be fifteen or sixteen," said Tapiwa. "A young man pays a few goats and some dollars for a wife and then takes his bride off to a place in the forest. After clearing the land they build a shelter, which is set on high stilts in order to protect themselves from animals."

As we drove past a dam, Tapiwa told me that we were almost

at our destination. Originally a natural water catchment area, the dam had been constructed to regulate the water supply and provide irrigation for crops all year round. It was refreshing to see beautiful rows of maize and vegetables in the fields in the middle of July, a month regarded as the hottest and driest in Zimbabwe.

We pulled into a compound where about a dozen men and women came out to meet us. They welcomed us to the shade of a shelter which was built on stilts just as Tapiwa had described. It was quite obvious that many of the elderly men were drunk.

A striking young woman with a shaved head and large earrings began the introductions in Shona. "First of all, I want to introduce myself. My name is Lydia Mola and I am Chief Mola's daughter. I am also the community health worker in the villages around here. Over there are my three children" – she pointed to some children playing in the sand nearby – "and that is my mother."

Lydia's mother did not stir or acknowledge our presence in any way. She sat cross-legged out in the sun, her shaved head shining, her sagging breasts touching her knees. Between her legs she nursed a gourd with a long spout which she was sucking, blowing out huge clouds of smoke. Lydia continued the introductions but I was not listening: my eyes were fixed on this extraordinary topless old lady. As I watched, a younger woman, who was also topless, sat down beside Lydia's mother and began sharing the gourd pipe with her.

From the aroma of the acrid smoke, I could tell they were smoking *mbanje*. Among the Tonga, this was a perfectly standard practice. The government could scarcely prevent it, so despite the prohibition against marijuana in the rest of the country, it was smoked openly in Omay, particularly by the women. Increasingly, the Tonga men preferred either traditional sorghum beer or the European variety.

After the introductions, Lydia took us around the irrigated crops.

"We harvest our crops three times a year," she said. "This means that for most of the year, we do not go home."

"What do you mean?" I asked.

"Most Tonga people have two homes: a shelter in the fields and a hut in the main compound. As soon as the seedlings come through, we move most of our belongings to the house in the fields."

The field homes, wooden lean-tos perched precariously on stilts about three metres off the ground, were very rough structures indeed. Reached by a ladder, they looked barely strong enough to support a single person, let alone an entire family, through a growing season.

"During the day we guard the crops against baboons and monkeys," continued Lydia. "At night, the elephants and the buffaloes come down to eat anything they can get hold of. An elephant can destroy a whole crop within minutes, so staying by our fields is a matter of survival."

Lydia showed me tins full of stones that the hapless farmers rattled at night when they heard an elephant moving near their fields. In theory, the elephant heard the strange noise and ran away. Sometimes it worked and sometimes it didn't, according to Lydia. A night's sound sleep by your fields could easily mean a season's hunger for your family.

"Do you ever go back home while the crops are growing? Even for one night?"

"Not really. Everyone knows when we have moved to the fields and they visit us here."

"But you have only one shelter on stilts. Where do your children sleep?"

"At night, my husband, my children and anyone who happens to be around climbs up the ladder to sleep. The floor is quite comfortable once you get used to it."

"But . . . what about privacy?"

"Privacy?" Lydia looked at me and then giggled. "Oh, you mean intimacy with my husband? Well, he is not always here, as he has other wives to visit. But if he is around, we wait until the children are asleep. And we can always send the older children back home to their grandmothers in the compound."

It was too hot to continue walking around the fields, so we returned to the shady shelter in the compound where Lydia offered us some *mahewu*. We were sipping it gratefully, when we heard a loud voice.

"More visitors from the president's office! More flash cars and flash clothes! Go away – we no longer want to listen to your promises!" a middle-aged man shouted as he limped towards us. He was tall with broad shoulders, but his left leg was skinny and almost useless – the legacy of polio I presumed – so that he had to support himself with a walking stick. He spoke furiously in Tonga, adding sentences of broken Shona, Ndebele and English.

"This is my husband," said Lydia, sheepishly. I could not hide my surprise. How could such a beautiful young woman be married to this elderly, abusive cripple?

"I am wife number four, the youngest and the most loved," said Lydia. Then she paused and lowered her voice. "You know, he has not visited his other three wives even once in the past three months." She held up three fingers for added emphasis. "I have tried to tell him to go and visit them, but he just will not go. He is hoping to make me pregnant because my youngest child is four years old now. But what he does not know is that I am on Depo-Provera. I do not need any more children."

"But why did you marry a man who is so much older than you are?"

"He approached my father, Chief Mola, for my hand. My father said that if he promised to work on our family's fields for at least three years, he could marry me. It was an agreement between the two of them. I had nothing to do with it."

"So it was a forced marriage?"

"Oh no," Lydia laughed. "I knew my husband and his family before I married him. Apart from his crippled leg, there is nothing wrong with him. He really is a good man despite the drunkenness that is making him so foolish just now. Believe me, he has never laid his hand on me. He still lives with me in the family compound and he has not taken another wife after marrying me."

She explained that women held a privileged position among the Tonga because it was a matriarchal society. Land and other possessions were inherited through the female line; when a chief died, for instance, the chieftainship was passed down to his sister's son. A man would live with his wife's family after their marriage. Each time he married again, he would live with the new wife's family for some time, and then divide his time between all his wives. This meant that a woman did not leave her family, as happened in the rest of Zimbabwe. In the end, most Tonga compounds were made up of senior women and their daughters.

"But our society is changing," said Lydia. "If I had married a young man who worked at one of the holiday resorts, I would have had to live with him in the workers' compound. Most of my friends have left our village to live with their husbands. But I could not do that because I am the chief's daughter."

While Lydia was talking to me, Tapiwa was trying to calm

down her husband and explain who we were. But the man would not believe that we were not government officers.

"You are Mugabe's people! Traitors who do not care for the Tonga people. We do not have clinics, schools or transport. But do you care? No, you do not! All you want to do is to come here and parade your flash cars. Look at this one," he pointed at me with his walking stick. "Sunglasses and a hat – as if she is a white lady. Whoever died from the sun?"

Everyone laughed and I did too. Lydia told me to ignore her husband. "He has had a few beers and he has probably smoked a little too much as well. He is harmless, really."

But her husband was warming to his topic. "We do not have enough grinding mills. Go to the nearest one today and see how many women wait for four or five days, just to get their maize ground. Imagine spending five days at a grinding mill! And what do these poor women eat while they're waiting? They have to roast the corn they brought there to grind into maize meal. By the time they come home, the sack is half-empty."

"That is true," Lydia said. "We desperately need a grinding mill. Walking fifteen to twenty kilometres with a bag of maize on your head and a baby on your back is really hard. Please help us and give us a grinding mill. The government cannot help, but I know that outside agencies are willing to support us."

In my notebook, I jotted down 'Grinding mill – a major priority' for my evaluation report. Not so long ago, white missionaries had come here with Bibles under their arms determined to save souls; now it was black or white aid workers equipped with socialist ideals and missionary-like zeal who saw themselves saving the Tonga.

"What about clinics?" I asked Lydia.

"There is only one clinic in this area and it services people from as far as forty kilometres away," she replied. "Sometimes I wish the clinic was not there. What is the point of a sick person being wheeled in a wheelbarrow over rough terrain for two days in the heat only to get to the clinic and be offered Aspirin? Even if someone is dying, the nurse at the clinic cannot take them to the nearest hospital, which is in Kariba."

"Yes. Remember what happened to Nyagande's daughter?" said a women who was drawing on a gourd pipe. "She was in labour for three days and finally her family hired a donkey to take her to the clinic. She fell off the donkey several times. At the clinic, there was no transport to take her to Kariba. A National Parks and Wildlife truck that happened to be passing, carrying some freshly culled animals, took her to Bumi Hills police camp. Already covered in blood from the meat, the poor woman was taken to Kariba Hospital in a police boat. She gave birth to the baby there and it survived – but the woman died. Then came the problem of bringing the body back to the village. Her family could not afford to pay for the transport, she was buried over there. That is unheard of in our tradition." The woman took a long, defiant pull at her gourd.

"Her husband brought the baby back," said Lydia, "but it soon died from lack of food. Would it not have been better for Nyagande's daughter to have died among her own people?"

The men joined in the conversation, arguing that clinics and hospitals were useless without the infrastructure to support them. "Tell the lady about what happened to Sophia's son," someone said to Tapiwa, and for the first time I saw Tapiwa's face change. He looked quite serious as he told me about the incident, while everyone listened.

"Sophia works as a tea lady and receptionist in our project offices in Siakobvu. She is one of the few Tonga women who can read and write. Her home is somewhere beyond Mayovhe, near the fishing camps in Kasvisva. As you can imagine, no buses service that part of the world.

"One morning a cousin of hers arrived at the Siakobvu offices to announce that Sophia's five-year-old son had died. The cousin had walked all afternoon and all night through dangerous forests to bring the news. Another messenger had set out to inform Sophia's husband, who works as a waiter at Tiger Bay, of the death of the boy. Meanwhile their relatives were already preparing the child's grave, because in this Omay heat a body must be buried within twenty-four hours.

"I decided to drive Sophia home, hoping that we would be in time for the burial. It did not take us too long to get to Sophia's village by car. We arrived just in time to see the body being carried out of the hut on a small stick-and-bark stretcher. Sophia began wailing and cuddled her son. Then she suddenly stopped crying and frantically began undressing the boy. She placed her hand on his chest and called out to me. I examined the child and my basic first aid training was enough to tell me that he was not dead at all, but in a coma. We rushed him to Bumi Hills and then to Kariba. By late afternoon a doctor was attending to him and told us that the boy was suffering from cerebral malaria. Three weeks later, Sophia brought her little Lazarus home."

Everyone took a deep breath. Some people shook their heads.

"Our people have very little knowledge of diseases and their symptoms," said Lydia.

"That is because when our parents and grandparents lived in the Zambezi valley, we were a very healthy people," said one of the men. "The white people destroyed us and now our own black brothers in government are making sure that we are completely forgotten."

I wrote all these problems down, although I was not sure what the head office far away in Australia could do. But I promised Lydia and the others, rather unconvincingly, that their problems were going to be passed on to the responsible authorities. Feeling guilty and helpless, I climbed into the four-wheel drive and waved goodbye. I think all of us, the Tonga, Tapiwa and I, knew that not much would change as a result of this visit.

◤▲▲◥

"We are booked into Bumi Hills Safari Lodge overnight," Tapiwa announced. "It is only thirty kilometres away. Tomorrow we will pick up Thomas from the office on our way back to Harare."

I nodded, and we drove west, towards the sunset. Before long, I was relaxing with a double gin and tonic on a comfortable chair overlooking the vast expanse of water spread out in front of me. Every so often, a speedboat full of tourists on their way out for sundowner drinks or their evening game-viewing would disturb the glassy surface of Lake Kariba.

Across the water, I could see the jagged shapes of dead trees which had once lined the banks of the Zambezi before the valley was flooded to make way for the lake. In the gathering twilight, the bleached branches looked like the frozen arms of skeletons thrust skywards. These were the trees under which the Tonga had sheltered when they fished the river, the trees that had provided firewood, building materials and traditional medicines for generations. I tried to think back to a time before the valley was flooded, imagining the sacred places where the Tonga people had been buried, the quiet places where their children played or learnt the art of fishing. I thought of the Tonga women sitting on the

219

shore smoking their pipes, telling old stories about the land and the river.

It was all gone now. The Tonga lived like fugitives in their own land. Lake Kariba was intended to be the showpiece of the Rhodesian Federation, producing hydroelectric power to drive the factories and towns of a brave new European society. But the federation had gone too and the African government did not have the guts to address the injustice that it had done to the Tonga, politely ignoring them instead. Nyaminyami, the river god, could no longer hear the Tonga people, living forgotten in the sick country of Omay. Soon they would blend into the ragged assortment of settlers and squatters whose shanties had begun to push up against the chocolate-box beauty of the lake.

From the verandah of the hotel, the tourists and I watched the animals come down to drink at the water. A variety of international accents surrounded me. In a couple of hours I would be all dressed up and ready for a five-course dinner served by smiling Tonga waiters.

In my mind I could see Lydia by her fields, climbing up into her rickety hut on stilts and preparing for a long night with the elephants.

CHAPTER 12

Songs at Sunset

IN THE WESTERN world families often get together at Christmas; it is the occasion when siblings forgive each other for past fights and begin new ones. My family had last been united at Charles's funeral. This August weekend, we were meeting to remember him as well as to finally accept that he existed in spirit form; our brother was now our protector, our ancestor, and tonight the ceremony of his second burial would take place.

In Shona culture, it is believed that when an adult dies his spirit wanders all over the place waiting to be united with the ancestors at a second burial ceremony; the ceremony is also a kind of homecoming for the spirit, who is reunited with his family. It was thus a time for celebration rather than mourning.

The most important ritual concerned the preparation of the *doro*, made of sorghum and maize meal, which was traditionally drunk at the ceremony. Very early in the morning, ten days before the ceremony, village elders and close relatives of our family had gathered in our granary where the red sorghum was stored, and announced to the ancestors that preparations for the second burial were to begin.

"We wish to be reunited with our son. He has been wandering

out in the forest for too long," said one of the elders. Women clapped and ululated as the grain was taken out of the hut and shown to everyone.

If my sisters or I had lived in the village, it would have been our responsibility to brew the beer. But as we all lived elsewhere, the task fell to our female cousins. They soaked several buckets of grain in water for three days until it showed signs of germinating. Then they drained away the water, dried the sorghum in the sun and then ground it into a powder. This powder had the same effect as yeast. Over the following seven days, our cousins, with the assistance of other female relatives, followed all the stages of brewing traditional beer. On the final day of the brew, some of this undiluted full-strength beer was stored in two clay pots placed on top of each other and sealed together with mud. A piece was broken off another clay pot and used as a cover. The set of pots was placed on a bench to make an altarlike stand in the granary; it symbolised Charles's spirit and had to be guarded overnight by the cousins who had brewed the beer.

The rituals surrounding the second burial also required Charles's widow, Rudo, to decide whether she wanted to remain single or be inherited by a male member of the family. According to tradition, Sydney was not a contender for her hand because he was older than Charles, which meant that he was a father figure to Rudo. Moreover, after Baba's death, Amai had rejected all our uncles and offered Sydney our father's possessions, thereby symbolically appointing him to our father's position. That way, she could remain a widow in the village under the patriarchal protection of her son. The situation would have been different if she had had no sons. Without a son, a widow faced considerable pressure to accept being inherited as a wife by one of her husband's brothers or cousins. In Rudo's case, her eldest son was still only a boy so all the cousins were going to try their luck, just in case Rudo felt that she needed a husband.

▲▲▲

Along with my sisters and sisters-in-law, I was sitting on Amai's verandah watching the sunset. As the sun sank lower in the sky, the village drummers began to warm the cowhide skins of their drums, carefully turning them in front of the flames of the fire because a drum must be warmed before it can sing its songs. The ceremony would begin once everyone had eaten. Just like at Charles's funeral, the *varoora* from my mother's maiden village were present and would provide all the labour needed during the ceremony, as well as singing, dancing and generally entertaining everyone.

"Tonight, you will dance to your husband's name," said Charity, pouring tonic water over Rudo's gin and ice. Three days before, Charity had left New York with her son, Munashe. Sipping gin and tonic in the village was certainly a long way from her diplomatic life at the United Nations, but I always envied the way Charity related to the villagers – at ease and very much at home with people she had not seen for years. But then again, Charity had had the opportunity of living in the village for the three years following our father's death. While the rest of us were packed off to boarding school, Charity stayed at home to assist Amai in brewing beer and selling it so she could earn enough money for our fees. My sisters and I would collect as many English novels as we could find and bring them home for her to read. Soon Charity became notorious for pausing from household tasks to read Mills and Boon whenever Amai was out of sight. She still has a scar where Amai once hit her with a piece of burning firewood when she caught Charity reading a novel during the crucial stirring of a pot of *sadza*.

It was mainly Charity's passion for reading that eventually made Amai send her back to boarding school. By that time, Phaina and Constance, our two older sisters, were teaching and nursing respectively, and the family finances were not so strained.

When we were children, I was always regarded as the weak, religious one while Charity was the outspoken, strong one. When she completed her secondary schooling, Charity briefly joined the liberation struggle, and with independence entered university to study politics and administration. She went on to join the Department of Foreign Affairs, and after four years in Brussels and a short period at home she was posted to New York. Her journey away from the village was complete.

"You will have to jump over Charles's possessions first before you choose a husband," said Vongai, who had flown in from Melbourne the evening before. Under her traditional wrap-around cloth, she wore a pair of skin-tight bicycle shorts; she planned to sneak off for her daily jog later on. "If you have slept with a man before this cleansing ceremony, you will fall over in front of everyone," she teased Rudo.

I sometimes felt sorry for our sisters-in-law; it was difficult for them to compete for status in a family of eight girls and they often felt threatened by our dominant role in the family.

Phaina tried to reassure Rudo. "That is the myth. No-one falls over these days," she said.

"Psychologically, you could feel guilty and trip over something," said Constance.

"Why should I feel guilty?" asked Rudo. "I have not been unfaithful to my late husband. I do not see why I cannot jump –

or even fly! – over his possessions."

"I knew a woman who jumped over her husband's belongings even though she knew she was already three months pregnant by someone else," Phaina said.

"What does it matter anyway?" said Vongai. "This ritual of jumping over a husband's possessions was created simply in order to keep women under male control." While everyone else drank alcohol, she was on her second litre of mineral water.

"Yes. Why is it that this rule only applies to women and not to men?" agreed Rumbi. "How many widowers have girlfriends or even get married before the second burial of their late wives?" She and Vongai shared Charity's outspokenness.

"You cannot change a custom overnight," I remarked.

"Yes, you can," said Vongai. She was about eight years my junior yet she spoke with so much more confidence than I did. "If we do not change these traditions, no-one will. That is why women have to be organised and fight these discriminatory practices. It that not correct?"

"These village practices are not going to change," said Rairo. "Ask Charity – she went to the Beijing Women's Conference, and they talked and talked for days about issues like this. But we have not seen any of their decisions filtering down to the grassroots women like us."

Everyone laughed at Rairo's description of herself as a 'grassroots woman'. "How many 'grassroots women' drink Western beer the way you are doing? How many of them have luxuries like you have?" asked Jessie.

"The grassroots women are over there," said Vongai, pointing to a line of five women carrying clay pots of beer to the men.

"I'd like another beer myself," said Rudo. I grabbed her one from the ice-filled cooler box, and the talking and drinking continued.

▲▲▲

After the sun had gone down, Simba lit a fire near the hut and prepared a barbecue. The *varoora* served us chicken and goat's meat with *sadza*. Sitting away from the crowd, my sisters and I shared many childhood reminiscences, especially about Charles. Nearby, our children played hide-and-seek in the moonlight. I could see my son Julian, back from Melbourne for the holidays, demonstrating the art of Australian Rules football to his village cousins; they had never seen the likes of this strange oval ball that refused to bounce the way they wanted it to.

There must have been about fifteen of my nieces and nephews altogether, including some of Charles's children from extra-marital relationships. Only two of his four girlfriends had come for the ceremony. Just like at the funeral, Rudo did not have any hard feelings towards these women; in fact, they were all talking together, laughing and sharing drinks.

After dinner, the drums started pounding and people began to dance. Phaina, being the oldest, instructed us to take turns in guarding the clay pots that symbolised Charles's spirit. My turn came shortly after midnight; I sat next to the pots and listened to the singing. No hymn books, no prearranged programme to follow – yet the songs flowed on uninterrupted, with never a moment of silence.

Of all the songs I heard that night, one in particular has stayed with me. One of my tall uncles began singing and then all the voices joined in as the song built to a crescendo:

VekwaNzenza!
Torai hama muende nayo kumatare
Ha! Avigwe kumusha.
Ndonovigwepi?
Ha-a! Ndovigwa kumusha.
Ndonovigwepi?
Harare, handidi!

'The Nzenza People!
Take your dead son home
To the burial place
Bury him at home.
Where will I be buried?
Ha-a! I was buried at home.
I rejected the cemetery in Harare!'

It was as if Charles himself was thanking us for honouring him with a fine burial in the village. Many people refused to be buried in the village these days because they had attained social position or wealth in Harare and preferred to be on show in the city cemeteries with big gaudy headstones. But with the AIDS epidemic, these more fashionable resting places were filling up quickly and bodies were now being buried less than a metre apart; mourners at a funeral virtually had to stand on adjacent burial plots, and when the rains came the earth would shift and many graves collapse.

Charles had been buried next to our father under the protective branches of a pair of thorn trees, looking out over the valley where our family had lived and died for many years. We could sit with him whenever we liked; nobody could tell us that the gates would be closing at sunset or that they would have to dig another hole almost on top of our brother. I wondered how the ancestral spirits could ever find peace in the chaos of the city graveyards.

Songs celebrating Charles's future in the ancestral world were sung throughout the night. The drums did not stop nor did the five drummers tire; later on, Sydney boasted that he had attracted the best drummers in the area.

At dawn, we all walked slowly to Charles's grave, singing as we went. Beer was poured over the shiny black serpentine of the headstone as women ululated. The oldest member of our extended family then welcomed the return of Charles's spirit.

"You are finally home, our dear son. Now you can sit with your ancestors and look after your family. Today, we will appoint one of your children to carry your name. We have completed all that is required of us and we now expect you to play your spiritual role. Great Antelope, you of the Vahera clan, we bid farewell once again to your physical presence and we welcome the spirit that will mediate our wishes to the Great Spirit on high."

After more singing and ululating at Charles's grave, we walked back to the homestead. As was the custom, Sydney then presented a fat ox to the people and announced that it was going to be slaughtered. This should have been Adam's job but he preferred to lock himself inside the house for this part of the ceremony. So four young men, who had married our cousins, produced sharp knives and an axe and set to work. After a few blows, blood spurted out and the huge beast fell onto the branches cut for that purpose.

It was only later, when I overheard them discussing it, that I realised that Julian and the other children had witnessed the slaughtering.

"It was like torture," said Munashe, in his heavy American accent.

"They should place the ox in an electric chair and kill it quick smart!" said Julian. For a while the group of children talked about the dead ox and how they felt sorry for it. But they stopped sympathising with the animal when Simba gave each of them a piece of meat to roast on the fire. "This is just like camping!" they shouted, as they tore at the burnt meat. Simba was urging the boys to eat a mixture of boiled blood and tendon, ladling out spoonfuls into their hands. "This is what makes you a man."

After the meat had been roasted and eaten, everyone gathered around the clay pots that had been guarded through the night. The uncles inspected them and announced to the people that the two pots were intact. If they had been cracked, it would have meant that Charles's spirit was unhappy about something.

After much clapping and ululating, Uncle Mujubheki lifted up the broken third pot and poured out the strong, undiluted beer. A gourd was passed around and everyone drank the beer as a final celebration for the return of Charles's ancestral spirit.

▰▰▰

Shortly after sunrise, the *varoora* brought out buckets of water, and people took the opportunity to wash their face and hands. A number of people started arriving for breakfast. It was the dry season and there wasn't enough food to eat in the villages; word had gone around about the ceremony, and everyone knew that it meant they could have a free breakfast, lunch and dinner. By 10 o'clock, there were about three or four hundred people sitting around Amai's front yard. The *varoora* made sweet tea in a huge drum and sliced up several loaves of bread; the disposable plates and cups that Charity and Vongai had brought with them came in handy.

After everyone had eaten, Uncle Mujubheki announced that the final ceremony was about to begin. The women and men were sitting quietly, apart from each other. My sisters and I sat with Rudo, close to the centre of the crowd.

"We want to cleanse our son's wife and appoint someone to carry his name," Uncle Mujubheki said. He brought out some things that had belonged to Charles: a pair of trousers, a shirt, a pair of shoes and a golf club. Quite a contrast to the old days, when the possessions would have been a bow and arrow, an axe and a walking stick.

Rudo's father then called her to him and spoke to her in very low tones. Although no-one could hear what he was saying, we all knew that he was telling Rudo to think about her conduct carefully before attempting to jump over Charles's possessions; to trip over and fall would be a great embarrassment to her and bring disgrace to her family. Rudo kept on nodding her head humbly while her father spoke. When he had finished, she curtsied to the audience and clapped her hands. She walked steadily towards Charles's possessions and then paused. There was dead silence. Suddenly, a simple step had taken on the gravity of an Olympic long jump.

"The moment of truth!" shouted a *varoora* and this seemed to break the tension. Rudo looked around at everyone, and clapped her hands again. She approached Charles's possessions confidently and skipped over them without wavering.

Her mother was the first to ululate in relief. For the elderly people, this was truly a moment of celebration: they shouted, clapped and cheered. Rudo had proved that she had not engaged in any sexual relations with a man since her husband's death. Rudo herself looked relieved, and as flushed as if she had just run a race.

"Imagine celebrating a two-year period of celibacy!" said Vongai. "If I were Rudo, I certainly would not have waited that long. Do you think she is really telling the truth?"

"What does it matter whether she is or she isn't? What she does with her body is no-one's business but hers," replied Charity.

Now that Rudo had proved her 'cleanliness', she was once again a potential bride. Uncle Mujubheki summoned her to the mat which had been placed in the centre of the yard. As Rudo came forward, wearing a white T-shirt and an elaborate headscarf that matched her wraparound cloth, you could see all the men admiring her. According to village standards, a plump woman was far more desirable than a thin one. A skinny wife was not beautiful, was not strong and healthy; being thin was potentially a sign that you had the HIV virus.

Five of our male cousins, aged between twenty and forty, were contending for Rudo. Uncle Mujubheki asked them to sit on a bench and wait for their turn in asking for her hand.

"Look at the one with sleepy eyes and uncombed hair," jeered one of the *varoora*, pointing at our cousin Joseph. "How can such a dirty old bachelor expect to inherit an urban wife? His eyes are so red. He looks like a drunken baboon!"

"Oh, but that one is better! Just look at Simeon – he got married last week and he is already fantasising about Rudo. And everyone knows he is struggling to feed even one wife. Such a skinny boy! How can he hope to maintain Rudo's weight?"

"I think the doctor should get the wife. Being a doctor, he probably knows how to handle older women," yet another *varoora* said, pointing at Peter. Peter was in his third year of medicine at university. His mother could not hide her anger; she did not want her twenty-three-year-old son to inherit Rudo. But

Peter was adamant that he would try his luck: "Why not? I will be a good young lover for Rudo as well as a good father to Charles's children!"

Poor Sydney was looking crestfallen. If he had been younger than Charles, today would have been his day. Tonight he would have smelt Rudo's expensive perfume in his sheets.

"I could easily change the rules," he said, meditatively stroking his chin. "Being a father figure need no longer mean that I cannot inherit my younger brother's widow. Tradition could begin to change right here!" But nobody took Sydney seriously, so he consoled himself with another jug of village beer.

"Death is cruel," said one toothless old man, shaking his head. "How can a man die and leave such a beautiful woman with such lovely fat brown legs to others? If only I was young!"

The *varoora* laughed and jeered at him and he pretended to chase one of them. Shaking his walking stick, he shouted that he was still man enough to give the woman ten children.

Uncle Mujubheki told the people to be quiet. Then he instructed Joseph, the oldest cousin, to carry a wooden bowl full of water to Rudo. Joseph took a few slow, measured steps towards the 'bride'. But then he paused, scratched his back and then started picking his nose nervously.

"Disgusting!" Vongai whispered.

"That one is a loser," Julian said in his broad Australian accent. I told him to keep quiet. Joseph finally knelt in front of Rudo and handed her the bowl of water. She smiled at him, accepted the bowl and, with one swift movement, threw the water away. There was a roar of laughter.

"Why did she do that?" asked Munashe.

"She is showing that she does not want to be married to him," explained Rairo.

"I do not blame her. That guy looks like he is very poor to me. Look at his bare feet and torn trousers. Without doubt, he's a peasant," said Julian.

"I would not want my mother to marry any of those men," said Kumbi, Rudo's ten-year-old son. He had been subdued all night and now he seemed very upset, glaring darkly at his mother's suitors. "In fact, I do not want her to marry anyone."

"Shhhh, children, be quiet," said an old woman. "Who are these noisy children who keep on insulting the audience by speaking in English? Why don't their mothers teach them to speak our language?"

We pretended not to have heard her. The second, third and fourth suitors each knelt before Rudo with their bowls and in each case Rudo threw the water away. Peter was the last contender. He was wearing nicely ironed jeans and a blue T-shirt. His hair was cut very short at the back and was twisted into dreadlocks at the front.

"Now that's a cool guy!" said Munashe. "Look at his Reeboks! He looks like a basketball player."

"Yes, if I were Mai Kumbi, I would definitely pick that man," agreed Julian. "He is so much better looking and cleaner than all the village guys. He's probably even got a car."

"My mum is not interested in him either – you wait and see. I wouldn't like to call that man Dad," said Kumbi, his eyes full of tears.

Julian and Munashe hugged him. "Don't worry, mate, your mum is rich. She can go back to Harare or even to Germany and choose any man she wants," said Julian reassuringly.

Peter seemed to be enjoying the attention. Before he picked up the bowl of water, he took a comb out of his pocket and gently combed the back of his head. Then he produced some moisturiser which he rubbed into his face before applying some lip balm. Everyone joked about this and laughed at him, but he took no notice. He stretched languidly and patted himself on the back. Picking up the bowl, he performed a little dance while singing Bob Marley's 'Three Little Birds'.

But by then the elderly people's patience had been stretched too far. "Do you want the woman or do you just want to continue acting?" asked one of the uncles.

"A man has to prove that he is worthy of the bride. And there are many ways to make a lasting impression," replied Peter. He went down on one knee, whispered something to Rudo sitting patiently on the mat and then kissed her on the cheek – something that was never done in public, especially in the village. "At least I can kiss the bride before I am accepted!"

Rudo giggled loudly. She accepted the bowl from Peter and then quickly threw the water in his face. There was another roar of laughter, mostly from the women.

"Life is so unfair! The love of my life will not take me. Are you sure this is what Charles would expect you to do?" Peter asked. But everyone could see that he was joking.

When all the laugher and commotion was over, I realised that our uncles were not at all pleased with Rudo's refusal to accept a new husband.

"Who does she think she is?" I heard Uncle Chakwanda mutter. "A woman of her age cannot live without a man."

I remembered how Amai had rejected all the uncles at my father's second burial. That was a much more dramatic situation, because Amai was a village woman with ten children to care for. After rejecting all her suitors, she had offered the bowl of water to Sydney and announced that he was going to be the father of the homestead.

Her co-wife, Mainini (small mother), was only twenty at the time and Amai would not let her jump over my father's possessions.

"I am the senior wife and if I jump, I do it for her as well. If I accept a man as my husband, I also accept on her behalf," Amai had argued. It was only much later that we children realised why Mainini had not jumped over Baba's possessions: six months after the ceremony, Mainini gave birth to a child whose father was the village school-teacher.

Now Amai called Kumbi out in front of the crowd and told him to sit on the mat. Rudo then offered him the bowl of water. The boy smiled as he washed his hands in it.

"Wow! This means Kumbi now owns the Mercedes Benz, the BMW, the house, the printing company and everything!" shouted Julian.

"He will have to wait until he turns eighteen," Munashe said, seriously.

"Eh, guys, don't get so excited. This is only a ceremony. All it means is that Mai Kumbi is now a free woman," Vongai explained.

The uncles grudgingly announced that the wishes of the widow had to be respected. They presented the golf club to Kumbi and all the women ululated. "The spirit has returned to the people. Charles's name lives among us," they said.

Uncle Mujubheki then announced that the main business was over; what was left was more eating, drinking, singing and dancing. But before the celebrations could continue, we saw a brown-clad figure approaching; behind him walked a group of women dressed in white and blue. It was Father Francis, come to hold mass at the homestead.

"But how can the Catholic priest hold mass at a second burial?

We are celebrating ancestral worship and not Jesus Christ," Uncle Mujubheki complained.

Amai quietly reminded him that although she worshipped the ancestors, she was still a Catholic. It was an honour to be visited by Father Francis on this particular day, she explained, and went over to welcome Father Francis and the women.

While his assistants set up a table for mass, Father Francis came over to greet my sisters and me. He then took our young sons over to a mango tree to hear their confessions. We watched the boys lining up. Father Francis did not expect my nieces, Farai and Mudiwa, to confess; the irony was that these two attended a Catholic boarding school and were the only genuine Catholics around.

"I am so glad that Vongai told me what to say beforehand," Julian said when he returned to the verandah. "All I said was that I was a bad boy who told many little lies and the priest believed me!"

"I said that I wished I could eat less. But in the States they give us such yummy food at school that I can't help eating too much," said Munashe, rubbing his fat little stomach. "I told the priest that I feel bad when I see how skinny some of the village boys are." The eight-year-old had put on a lot of weight since moving to New York.

After he had heard the confessions of all the boys, Father Francis invited everyone present to attend mass in front of Amai's hut. While several of the village men and a few women sat just a few metres away drinking beer, Father Francis preached for a good half-hour, reminding us that the important thing was to be united with the Lord after death.

When Father Francis finally left, Adam accompanied him halfway up the hill.

"Those two are probably related," Vongai said.

"No, they are not," said Julian. "Father Francis said he was Irish and Adam's ancestors were Scottish."

"Irish or Scottish, they are both white men. The only difference between those two is that one is celibate and the other one is not!" said Charity.

"How do you know what Father Francis does with his body? Only God knows that," replied Vongai.

"Leave them alone," I said.

◤▲▲

As the afternoon drew to a close, Amai and Sydney were sitting on the verandah drinking cold Zambezi Lager with the rest of us. Whenever they wanted bottled beer, as a change from the traditional brew, they would sneak away from the crowd so that they would not have to share the beer with everyone else.

Sydney was very pleased with himself. He told us that he felt like a chief because everything at the ceremony had gone according to plan.

"Not only that, but Father Francis came to bless us too. It all goes to show that although I have lost Rudo as a second wife, I am still a very important man in this area and even Father Francis knows it."

"It's going to be a beautiful evening," said Adam coming out of the house to join us. "I am going to climb the mountain before the sun goes down."

I said I needed some fresh air and would go with him.

"It's not a good idea to exercise after a hot day," Charity said. She was pouring glasses of chilled wine for Rudo and herself; Vongai was sipping a big mug of herbal tea.

But after two days with so many people around, I felt that climbing Dengedza would give me a chance to unwind. Dengedza was about two kilometres from the homestead, but it towered over us with its huge rocks and fortresslike cliffs. As a child, I had heard many scary stories about the mountain. It was rumored to be home to hyenas, leopards and even lions, and it was said that, late at night, the spirits of the ancestors who lived there could be heard celebrating a good harvest. I had never dared climb Dengedza, until Adam came to the village with his adventurous Western outlook and the mystery of the mountain seemed to disappear.

It took us about forty minutes to climb Dengedza. I liked to come up here at sunset, sit on the big rock at the summit and watch the sun go down. I could hear the women singing in our homestead, their voices echoing up beautifully. Far below, I could see the herd boys bringing the cattle back to the kraal for the night and hear the cow bells clanking. To the east, beyond the cleared land of our village, was the deep, dark forest of the wild country where no-one had yet settled.

An eagle drifted on the thermals high above, sending out its eerie sonar call to locate its prey, and field mice and rock rabbits scurried between the craggy granite outcrops around us. A baboon barked somewhere far away. Soon dozens of little squirrels came sniffing around us, investigating these intruders in their realm. It was unbelievably peaceful.

Few people ventured up here; most of the villagers were content to look up occasionally from their toil in the fields to contemplate the talismanic mountain where the ancestors reposed. Once, like them, I had unthinkingly accepted the power of Dengedza. Now, full of Western learning and scepticism, I had to climb the mountain to feel impressed by it, crashing up through the undergrowth, putting families of quail to flight. And I didn't even know what to say to the ancestors when I got to the top.

I knew that it was good to be back home. But I had to accept the inevitable – I could never live in the village again. At the end of this weekend, my sisters and I would all climb back into our four-wheel drives and return to Harare; some of us would then travel on to cold, rainy cities in Europe, Australia or the States, where we would not hear Shona spoken for months on end. I could not help wondering how much longer our homestead would exist; gradually, the village and all its people, myself included, were being swallowed up by modernity.

But there is a Shona belief that you will always return to the place where your mother buried a piece of your umbilical cord shortly after your birth. Amai buried mine near the village, so from time to time, according to tradition, I would have to return to lay a stone on the spot. Sitting on top of Dengedza, listening to the celebratory songs drifting up the mountain, I comforted myself with the reassuring thought that however far my journey took me, I would always be connected to this place.

LONELY PLANET JOURNEYS

JOURNEYS is a unique collection of travel writing – published by the company that understands travel better than anyone else.

It is a series for anyone who has ever experienced – or dreamed of – the magical moment when they encountered a strange culture or saw a place for the first time. They are tales to read while you're planning a trip, while you're on the road or while you're in an armchair, in front of a fire.

Lonely Planet guidebooks have always gone beyond providing simple nuts-and-bolts information, so it is a short step to JOURNEYS, a new series of outstanding titles that explore our planet through the eyes of a fascinating and diverse group of international travellers.

JOURNEYS books catch the spirit of a place, illuminate a culture, recount a crazy adventure, or introduce a fascinating way of life. They always entertain, and always enrich the experience of travel.

FULL CIRCLE
A South American Journey
Luis Sepúlveda (translated by Chris Andrews)

'A journey without a fixed itinerary' in the company of Chilean writer Luis Sepúlveda. Extravagant characters and extraordinary situations are memorably evoked: gauchos organising a tournament of lies, a scheming heiress on the lookout for a husband, a pilot with a corpse on board his plane . . . Part autobiography, part travel memoir, *Full Circle* brings us the distinctive voice of one of South America's most compelling writers.

WINNER 1996 Astrolabe – Etonnants Voyageurs award for the best work of travel literature published in France.

THE GATES OF DAMASCUS
Lieve Joris (translated by Sam Garrett)

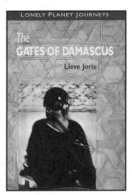

This best-selling book is a beautifully drawn portrait of day-to-day life in modern Syria. Through her intimate contact with local people, Lieve Joris draws us into the fascinating world that lies behind the gates of Damascus. Hala's husband is a political prisoner, jailed for his opposition to the Assad regime; through the author's friendship with Hala we see how Syrian politics impacts on the lives of ordinary people.

Written after the Gulf War, *The Gates of Damascus* offers a unique insight into the complexities of the Arab world.

IN RAJASTHAN
Royina Grewal

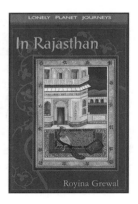

As she writes of her travels through Rajasthan, Indian writer Royina Grewal takes us behind the exotic facade of this fabled destination: here is an insider's perceptive account of India's most colourful state. *In Rajasthan* discusses folk music and architecture, feudal traditions and regional cuisine . . . Most of all, it focuses on people – from maharajas to camel trainers, from politicians to itinerant snake charmers – to convey the excitement and challenges of a region in transition.

ISLANDS IN THE CLOUDS
Travels in the Highlands of New Guinea
Isabella Tree

This is the fascinating account of a journey to the remote and beautiful Highlands of Papua New Guinea and Irian Jaya: one of the most extraordinary and dangerous regions on the planet. The author travels with a PNG Highlander who introduces her to his intriguing and complex world, which is changing rapidly as it collides with twentieth-century technology and the island's developing social and political systems. *Islands in the Clouds* is a thoughtful, moving book, full of insights into a region that is rarely noticed by the rest of the world.

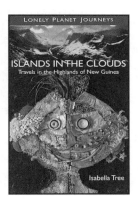

KINGDOM OF THE FILM STARS
Journey into Jordan
Annie Caulfield

Kingdom of the Film Stars is a travel book and a love story. With honesty and humour, Annie Caulfield writes of travelling in Jordan and falling in love with a Bedouin with film-star looks.

The author offers fascinating insights into the country – from the tent life of traditional women to the hustle of downtown Amman. *Kingdom of the Film Stars* unpicks tight-woven Western myths about the Arab world, presenting cultural and political issues within the intimate framework of a compelling love story.

LOST JAPAN
Alex Kerr

Lost Japan draws on the author's personal experiences of Japan over thirty years. Alex Kerr takes his readers on a backstage tour, exploring different facets of his involvement with the country: friendships with Kabuki actors, buying and selling art, studying calligraphy, exploring rarely visited temples and shrines . . .

The Japanese edition of this book was awarded the 1994 Shincho Gakugei Literature Prize for the best work of non-fiction: the first time a foreigner has won this prestigious award.

THE RAINBIRD
A Central African Journey
Jan Brokken (translated by Sam Garrett)

The Rainbird is a classic travel story. Following in the footsteps of famous Europeans such as Albert Schweitzer and H.M. Stanley, Jan Brokken journeyed to Gabon in central Africa. A kaleidoscope of adventures and anecdotes, *The Rainbird* brilliantly chronicles the encounter between Africa and Europe as it was acted out on a side-street of history. It is also the compelling, immensely readable account of the author's own travels in one of the most remote and mysterious regions of Africa.

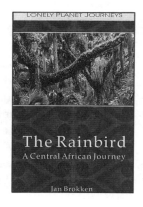

SEAN & DAVID'S LONG DRIVE

Sean Condon

Sean and David are young townies who have rarely strayed beyond city limits. One day, for no good reason, they set out to discover their homeland, and what follows is a wildly entertaining adventure that covers half of Australia. Highlights include the weekly Hair Wax Report and a Croc-Spotting with Stew adventure.

Sean Condon has written a hilarious, offbeat road book that mixes sharp insights with deadpan humour and outright lies.

SHOPPING FOR BUDDHAS

Jeff Greenwald

Here in this distant, exotic land, we were compelled to raise the art of shopping to an experience that was, on the one hand, almost Zen – and, on the other hand, tinged with desperation like shopping at Macy's or Bloomingdale's during a one-day-only White Sale.

Shopping for Buddhas is Jeff Greenwald's story of his obsessive search for the perfect Buddha statue. In the backstreets of Kathmandu, he discovers more than he bargained for . . . and his souvenir-hunting turns into an ironic metaphor for the clash between spiritual riches and material greed. Politics, religion and serious shopping collide in this witty account of an enlightening visit to Nepal.

RELATED TITLES FROM LONELY PLANET

Zimbabwe, Botswana & Namibia

This comprehensive guide provides down-to-earth advice for independent travellers on any budget. Containing detailed information on the colourful history and culture of the many peoples of the region, this guide is a must for all who intend to travel there.

Zimbabwe, Botswana & Namibia travel atlas

Make your journey to the spectacular countries of Zimbabwe, Botswana and Namibia with the handiest, most accurate maps available.

Africa on a shoestring

This all-time classic guide to travel on this fascinating continent is packed with essential information every traveller needs before embarking on a trip from Marrakesh to Cape Town.

Central Africa

Journeying to Central Africa, the least visited area of Africa, requires a great deal of organisation and a reliable guide book. This guide is packed with hard-to-get information for a safe and enjoyable visit.

East Africa

East Africa's diverse landscape, exotic wildlife and fascinating people make for an unforgettable experience. This guide book has all the details an independent traveller needs.

North Africa

This is the most extensive guide to the Maghreb – Morocco, Algeria, Tunisia and Libya – and it's full of reliable travel information for every budget.

West Africa

West Africa is the vibrant heart of traditional African art, music and culture. Explore it easily with this comprehensive guide book, essential for every independent traveller, no matter what the budget.

Also available:

Arabic (Egyptian) phrasebook, Arabic (Moroccan) phrasebook, Ethiopian (Amharic) phrasebook, Swahili phrasebook

PLANET TALK

Lonely Planet's FREE quarterly newsletter

Every issue of PLANET TALK is packed with up-to-date travel news and advice including:

- a letter from Lonely Planet founders Tony and Maureen Wheeler
- travel diary from a Lonely Planet author – find out what it's really like out on the road
- feature article on an important and topical travel issue
- a selection of recent letters from our readers
- the latest travel news from all over the world
- details on Lonely Planet's new and forthcoming releases

To join our mailing list contact any Lonely Planet office.

LONELY PLANET PUBLICATIONS

Australia: PO Box 617, Hawthorn 3122, Victoria
tel: (03) 9819 1877 fax: (03) 9819 6459
e-mail: talk2us@lonelyplanet.com.au

USA: Embarcadero West, 155 Filbert St, Suite 251,
Oakland, CA 94607
tel: (510) 893 8555 TOLL FREE: 800 275-8555
fax: (510) 893 8563 e-mail: info@lonelyplanet.com

UK: 10 Barley Mow Passage, Chiswick, London W4 4PH
tel: (0181) 742 3161 fax: (0181) 742 2772
e-mail: 100413.3551@compuserve.com

France: 71 bis rue du Cardinal Lemoine, 75005 Paris
tel: 1 44 32 06 20 fax: 1 46 34 72 55
e-mail: 100560.415@compuserve.com

World Wide Web: Lonely Planet is now accesible via the World Wide Web. For travel information and an up-to-date catalogue, you can find us at http://www.lonelyplanet.com/

THE LONELY PLANET STORY

Lonely Planet published its first book in 1973 in response to the numerous 'How did you do it?' questions Maureen and Tony Wheeler were asked after driving, bussing, hitching, sailing and railing their way from England to Australia.

Written at a kitchen table and hand collated, trimmed and stapled, *Across Asia on the Cheap* became an instant local bestseller, inspiring thoughts of another book.

Eighteen months in South-East Asia resulted in their second guide, *South-East Asia on a shoestring*, which they put together in a backstreet Chinese hotel in Singapore in 1975. The 'yellow bible' as it quickly became known to backpackers around the world, soon became *the* guide to the region. It has sold well over half a million copies and is now in its 8th edition, still retaining its familiar yellow cover.

Today there are over 180 titles, including travel guides, walking guides, language kits & phrasebooks, travel atlases and travel literature. The company is one of the largest travel publishers in the world. Although Lonely Planet initially specialised in guides to Asia, we now cover most regions of the world, including the Pacific, North America, South America, Africa, the Middle East and Europe.

The emphasis continues to be on travel for independent travellers. Tony and Maureen still travel for several months of each year and play an active part in the writing, updating and quality control of Lonely Planet's guides.

They have been joined by over 70 authors and 170 staff at our offices in Melbourne (Australia), Oakland (USA), London (UK) and Paris (France). Travellers themselves also make a valuable contribution to the guides through the feedback we receive in thousands of letters each year.

The people at Lonely Planet strongly believe that travellers can make a positive contribution to the countries they visit, both through their appreciation of the countries' culture, wildlife and natural features, and through the money they spend. In addition, the company makes a direct contribution to the countries and regions it covers. Since 1986 a percentage of the income from each book has been donated to ventures such as famine relief in Africa; aid projects in India; agricultural projects in Central America; Greenpeace's efforts to halt French nuclear testing in the Pacific; and Amnesty International.

'I hope we send the people out with the right attitude about travel. You realise when you travel that there are so many different perspectives about the world, so we hope these books will make people more interested in what they see.'

— **Tony Wheeler**